NIGHT SCHOOL

VOLUME I

THE SWORN AND SECRET GRIMOIRE

Night School: Volume I.
The Sworn and Secret Grimoire
Copyright © 2021 Jake Stratton-Kent
Interior images redrawn by S. Aldarnay and Dis Albion.

ISBN 978-1-914166-07-5 (Hardcover)
ISBN 978-1-914166-08-2 (Paperback)

A catalogue for this title is available from the British Library.
10 9 8 7 6 5 4 3 2 1

Hardcover edition printed by Biddles, Norfolk.

First published in 2021
Hadean Press
West Yorkshire
England

www.hadeanpress.com

NIGHT SCHOOL

VOLUME I

THE SWORN AND SECRET GRIMOIRE

By the

MASTER ARBATEL

Translated for our age by

COUNT ABAKA

ACKNOWLEDGEMENTS

In no particular order: Chris Carr for extensive distant technical support, sometimes on consecutive days and, along with S. Aldarnay, for mighty assistance in the graphics department. Erzebet Barthold for her continuing faith and support. Joseph Peterson for his selfless online archivism and so much fabulous hardcopy. Stephen Skinner and David Rankine for stoking the grimoire revolution. Aleister Crowley for what he got right, and his near forgotten encouragement of the art of ritual composition. Rob Rider Hill for reading and enthusing over my various screeds pre-publication. Frater Acher for new information regarding Olympic Spirit sigils. My readers and supporters for their encouragement and enabling me to live to write. Conference organisers including Gary Nottingham; Liz Williams and Trevor Jones; James and Sally North for similar support. Apologies to anyone I may have forgotten or omitted in the rush for a speedy release of this necessary work.

CONTENTS

INTRODUCTION

THE SECRET GRIMOIRE OF TURIEL

This work was initially planned as a slightly re-edited presentation of the *Secret Grimoire of Turiel* in order to make available a simple, hands on, get you started workbook of grimoire magic. On setting down to work, various problems made themselves apparent, altering the anticipated approach. Firstly, *Turiel* is, more or less, a forgery. This has been suspected in the past; the cover story given by 'Marius Malchus' is more likely fictional than factual. However, as Peterson and others have shown, *Turiel* derives from another 'forgery', whose author – self-confessed – was Frederick Hockley, resident-in-chief of a grimoire copying workshop in 19th century London. Hockley's text, compiled from older sources, is *The Complete Book of Magic Science*. Exhibiting several differences, it has a slightly fuller ritual process and a better handling of the incenses and other materials. However, useful as that is, simply appropriating these to *Turiel* is not sufficient.

What is attractive about *Turiel* is its apparent simplicity, with a complete and comparatively easily executed process, and a semblance, at least, of a spirit hierarchy neither biblically angelic nor dangerously demonic. The presentation simply requires a different approach. So, this is not a 'critical edition' of *Turiel* or anything of the kind, nor is it an academic work. It is closer to a reforging of Hockley's well-conceived but problematic 'forgery', riffing on *Turiel* but drawing in other compatible material to fulfil potential neither version really does. This involves correcting and expanding existing parts, employing better sources where necessary, as well as some replacements and expansion adding emphasis to some existing strong points and potentials. It is a workbook for modern grimoirists, employing the all-but-lost but deeply appropriate art of grimoire forging from actual grimoire materials.

OVERVIEW OF *TURIEL*

Part One: I. sundry prayers, benedictions, consecrations and exorcisms; II. Invocations for the days of the week; III. characters and perfumes of the Lords of the Seven Planets.

The material in Part One I presents the reader with materials for the preliminary stages of grimoire workings. It is essentially unproblematic from an editorial perspective; some better readings have been supplied. In II we receive a series of talismans and invocations for the days of the week. The invocations in fact represent a great strong point of the grimoire, being more atmospheric than the generality of Solomonic conjurations. They almost compare with the planetary rites of the *Picatrix*, where the 'mood' of each planet is emphasised; they are evocative of the individual planetary powers rather than the uniform 'biblical' flavour often encountered in Solomonic ritual. The talismans are more problematic as only some in *Turiel* resemble – never match – those in Hockley, while others are quite different. Hockley's also contains inscriptions of names in the double circle surrounding the central motif, which are all omitted in *Turiel*. As will become clear shortly, there is no reason even to trust *Turiel*'s attribution of the unmatched talismans, nor the rendering given of any of them. For different reasons, my solution does not involve drawing on Hockley either.

With the perfumes, major issues arise. Firstly, the order of the planets is completely arbitrary, it bears no relation to the days of the week previously employed, nor yet is it the so-called Chaldean order. Saturn appears first, conventionally enough, but is followed by Mars, then the Moon, Jupiter, Mercury, Venus and finally the Sun. This does not follow Hockley, who gives them in order of the days beginning with Sunday. Eccentric as this is, it is but the beginning of the difficulties in this section. Firstly, to seasoned grimoire hounds, the incenses – but not their attributions – are recognisable from usage elsewhere, including the often maligned *Petit Albert*, but never in such a mangled state as here. Plants and aromatics are misidentified and omitted; in short, the entire section is inoperable. Comparison with Hockley shows that while the planets have been disordered, the incenses retain the order in which Hockley gave them, so that, for example, the solar incense in *Turiel* is actually an incense of Saturn.

The problem is to an extent academic, since no editor of this work, myself included, encourages the reader to employ these incenses – quite the opposite. Their employment of many animal parts militates strongly against them. However, it is illustrative of the issues involved in relying on the text as it stands. For the sake of completeness I have restored the recipes via *Royal MS. 17A xlii*, along with a selection of alternatives for practical use rather than literary precision. Meanwhile the sigils of the Olympic Spirits accompanying the incenses in *Turiel* contain inexplicable additions and changes from the *Arbatel*, whose forms I have preferred here. Two points concerning these require mention. The *Turiel* version appears to be an elaboration on sigils accompanying Robert Turner's translation, which includes unaccountable additions and changes. I have preferred the form in the original Latin edition. These, it has been shown though Frater Acher's research, are monograms employing the Nine Chambers cipher. However, the curved lines in the Phul sigil (there are two in the Latin edition) do suggest some other inspiration at work, as the cipher only produces angular forms. This shape is more apt to a lunar sigil and doubles down on my preference here.

The casual observer might assume these to represent the flip side of the previously given talismans. Comparison with Hockley however shows the Olympic seals paired with an obverse containing various Solomonic angels. This approach, while commending itself to collation by crazy magicians whose tables ignore distinctions like different systems, requires a different approach here.

Two principal solutions present themselves:

1) The incenses accompanying the sigils match those the *Petit Albert* uses to consecrate planetary talismans. These have two sides: one has an image of the appropriate planetary god ('Olympic' deities), the other the magic square of the planet. It is highly likely that Hockley was well aware of this.

2) A similar combination, Olympic sigil on one side, magic square on the other, already appears in larger collections of pentacles (clumsily collating 'Paracelsian' into 'late-Solomonic'). Adding the sigil to the previous solution is more elegant and appropriate for the purposes of the present work. Here I have taken the planetary

images from *Le Grand Albert*, rather than those from its 'petit' cousin, for a variety of reasons, greater ease of copying among them, with the sigil added and with the squares on the reverse. Note well, numbers are to be written in order beginning with one, not copied line by line, as an auto-inductive technique.

Part Two: I. Containing invocations, conjurations, and exorcisms of the Band of Spirits; II Spirits, Messengers and Intelligences of the Seven Planets.

In Part Two the text firstly returns to delivering a readily followable ritual procedure; I shall be discussing grimoire ritual structure in detail later on in order to facilitate access to this and similar materials from elsewhere. Following this is one of the other major issues with *Turiel* as it stands; though by no means restricted to it, Hockley and numerous MS compilers do the same. It introduces us to the Olympic Spirits, who represent as it were an alternative to more 'biblical' themes in the Solomonic books. To be plain, the Olympic Spirits derive from Paracelsian revolutions in grimoire culture; they are not the angels of the Solomonic works. In the original presentation in the *Arbatel*, Olympic Spirits took the place of the angels. Being collated with them, while often done, misrepresents the *Arbatel*. While I have retained them herein, they are rather anachronistic from various perspectives, both Paracelsian and modern. I have also added the plainly more appropriate material from the *Arbatel* which does relate to the Olympic spirits. In short, there is no proper relationship between the angel Turiel and the Olympic spirit of Jupiter. It was at this juncture of my re-examining the grimoire that I realised my project was not and could not be a simple re-presentation of the *Secret Grimoire of Turiel* and would also break with Hockley. My purpose rather was to provide a grimoire for working with the Olympic Spirits, restoring the link with non-Solomonic strands of the grimoires.

Invocations, Interrogations, License to Depart and form of the
Bond of the Band of Spirits.

This comprises further presentation of useable ritual material, specific however more to Solomonic than Paracelsian and Olympic forms of the planetary hierarchy.

The Rites: further details regarding the Lords of the Planets.

This represents a massively condensed survey of the Olympic Spirits from the *Arbatel,* which I have instead incorporated in more complete form at various points of the reforged grimoire.

The Times: Time of Planetary Hours (Day);
Time of Planetary Hours (Night)

Here two tables of hours are given, without instructions, which unfortunately leaves open the possibility of confusing the hours of the clock with planetary hours, which is not the case. Again, I have rectified this omission with a modern and clarified account of the process and its meaning. Curiously enough, the grimoires frequently assume familiarity with the calculations required, but very rarely include them. In texts such as *The Secrets of Albertus Magnus*, modern editors omit his account of them, replacing them with an attractive but inadequate diagram instead.

HOW TO UNDERSTAND THE OLYMPIC SPIRITS

...In the belief of the ancients, the world is governed by seven secondary causes *–secundii*, as Trithemius calls them ['*De Septem Secundiis*', id est, *Intelligentiis, sive Spiritibus, Orbes post Deum Moventibus: Coloniae, 1567.* Waite's note] – which are the universal forces designated by Moses under the plural name of Eloïm, gods. These forces, analogous and contrary to one another, produce equilibrium by their contrasts and rule the movement of the spheres. The Hebrews termed them the seven great archangels, giving them the names of Michael, Gabriel, Anael, Samael, Zadkiel and Oriphiel. The Christian Gnostics named the last four Uriel, Barachiel, Sealtiel and Jehudiel. Other nations attributed to these spirits the government of the seven chief planets, and assigned to them the names of their chief divinities. All believed in their relative influence; astronomy divided the antique heaven between them and allotted the seven days of the week to their successive rule. Such is the reason of the various Ceremonies of the magical week and the septenary cultus of the planets (Eliphas Levi: *Transcendental Magic* II. VII.)

In other words, in appropriate contexts, the term Elohim represents the gods of the planets and the seven-day week, whether in the form of appropriate angels **or otherwise**. This understanding – as Syrian in origin as it is Jewish – underpins the Paracelsian usage of 'Olympians' and 'Olympic spirits'. It is the basis and origin of the planetary magic of the grimoires. In the understanding of the syncretic movements that shaped 'Western' Magic in Late Antiquity, and at various stages in the history of the grimoires, the Solomonic

Angels, the Greco-Roman gods of the planetary week, and the Olympic Spirits of Paracelsian tradition represent different cultural interpretations of the exact same principal characters.

While this may not represent Jewish understanding at all, it nevertheless explains the way other forms of thought expressed themselves. Also, as should be clear, I am not proposing to employ the Solomonic Angels in the reforging process. The Paracelsian phase of grimoire production remains Christian of course, however the 'old gods' are essentially rehabilitated in the form of 'Olympic Spirits'. So too various other rapprochements are made with earlier lore (see the *Arbatel*) which are not a feature of Solomonic works, which tend to demonise pagan forms. There are other ways in which Paracelsian magical thought – including its understanding of the spirits and their spheres of operation – differs massively from more familiar 'Qabalism' and Solomonic alike. Considerations such as these however would take us too far from the objects of this supposed 'beginners' manual. One might add that no real occult primer has ever really started at the 'shallow end' anyway, but it is traditional to make and maintain the pretence.

THE SWORN AND SECRET GRIMOIRE

BOOK ONE: PART ONE

OBSERVATIONS and method of Invoking related with great pains and diligent research.

Retire thyself Seven Days free from all company and fast and pray from sunset to sunrise. Rise every morning at Seven of the clock, and the three days previous to the Work fast upon bread and water and humble thyself before Almighty God. Watch and pray all night before the Work.

And on the day before draw the lines of the Circle in a fair place and let the diameter of the Circle be 9 feet. Wash thyself the same day quite clean.

Make the pentacles forthwith and provide the other things necessary, with Purifications and Incensing. Then being clothed in pure Vestments and having covered the Altar and lighted the candles begin about half an hour before sunrise on the Day assigned for the Work and say with great Devotion as follows:

First Morning Prayer: Almighty and Most Merciful Father I beseech Thee that Thou wilt vouchsafe favourably to hear me at this time whilst I make my humble prayer and Supplication unto Thee. I confess unto Thee O Lord Thou hast justly punished me for my manifold sins and offences but Thou hast promised at what time soever a sinner doth repent of his sins and wickedness Thou wilt pardon and forgive him and turn away the remembrance of them from before Thy face.

Purge me therefore O Lord and wash me from all my offences in the Blood of Jesus Christ that, being pure and clothed in the Vestments of Sanctity, I may bring this Work to perfection, through Jesus our Lord who liveth and reigneth with Thee in the Unity of the Holy Ghost. Amen.

Sprinkle thyself with Holy Water and say: Asperges me Domine hysope, et mundabor, Lavabis me, et super nivem dealbabor.

Hail O Mighty God, for in Thy power alone abideth the Key to all exorcising of Principalities, Powers, Thrones, Angels and Spirits. Amen.

Then bless your Girdle, saying:

O God Who by the breath of Thy nostrils framed Heaven and Earth and wonderfully disposed all things therein in six days, grant that this now brought to perfection by Thine unworthy servant may be by Thee blessed and receive Divine virtue, power and Influence from Thee that everything therein contained may fully operate according to the hope and confidence of me Thine unworthy servant through Jesus Christ our Lord and Saviour. Amen.

Asperges me, Domine, hyssopo et mundabor, Lavabis me, et super nivem dealbabor.

Miserere mei, Deus, secundum magnam misericordiam tuam. Gloria Patri et Filio et Spiritui Sancto Sicut erat in principio, et nunc, et semper, et in saecula saeculorum. Amen.

The Blessing of the Light:

I bless thee in the Name of the Father. O Holy, Holy Lord God, Heaven and Earth are full of Thy Glory, before Whose face there is a bright shining light forever; bless now, O Lord, I beseech Thee, these creatures of light which Thou hast given for the Kindly use of man that they, by Thee being sanctified, may not be put out or extinguished by the power, malice, or filthy darkness of the devil, but may shine forth brightly and lend their assistance to this my Work, through Jesus Christ our Lord. Amen.

Then say, Asperges me, etc.

Consecration of the Sword:

O Great God Who art the God of strength and fortitude and greatly to be feared, bless, O Lord, this Instrument that it may be a terror unto the Enemy, and therewith I may fight with and over-come all phantasms and oppositions of the Enemy, through the influence and help of Thy most Holy Mighty Name, On, Saint Agla, and in the Cross of Jesus Christ our only Lord. Amen.

Be thou blessed and consecrated in the Name of the Father, Son, and Holy Ghost.

Asperges me, etc.

Benediction of the Lamens (Symbols. Circles):

O God Thou God of my Salvation I call upon Thee by the mysteries of Thy most holy Name, On, Saint Agla, I worship and beseech Thee by Thy Names El, Elohim, Elohe, Zebaoth, and by Thy Mighty Name Tetragrammaton, Saday, that Thou wilt be seen in the power and force of these Thy most holy names so written filling them with divine virtue and Influence through Jesus Christ our Lord.

Benediction of the Pentacles:

Eternal God which, by Thy Holy Wisdom, hast caused great power and virtue to lie hidden in the characters and Holy Writings of Thy Spirits and Angels, and hast given unto man that with them, faithfully used, power thereby to work many things; bless these, O Lord, framed and written by the hand of me Thine unworthy servant that being filled with divine virtue and Influence by Thy Commands, O Most Holy God, they may shew forth their virtue and power to Thy praise and Glory through Jesus Christ our Lord. Amen.

I bless and consecrate you in the Name of the Father, the Son, and the Holy Ghost, the God of Abraham, Isaac, and Jacob.

Asperges me, etc. Amen.

Benediction of the Garment:

O Holy, blessed and Eternal Lord God Who art the God of purity and delightest that our souls should appear before Thee in clean and pure and undefiled Vestments being cleansed, blessed, and consecrated by Thee, I may put them on, being therewith clothed I may be whiter than snow both in soul and body in Thy presence this day, in and through the merit, death, and passion of our only Lord and Saviour Jesus Christ, Who liveth and reigneth with Thee in the Unity of the Holy Spirit, ever one God, world without end. The God of Abraham, Isaac and Jacob bless thee, purge thee, and make thee pure, and be thou clean in the Name of the Father, Son and Holy Ghost. Amen.

In this Thy Holy Sign O God, I fear no evil. By Thy Holy Power, and by this Thy Holy Sign all evil doth flee.

By Thy Holy Name and Thy Power which Secret was revealed to Moses, through the Holy Names written in this Book, depart far from me all ye workers of iniquity.

Bless, O Lord, I beseech Thee, this place and drive away all evil and wickedness far from it. Sanctify and make it become meet and convenient for Thy Servant to finish and bring to pass therein his desires, through Jesus Christ our Lord, Amen.

Be thou blessed and purified in the Name of the Father, Son, and Holy Ghost. Amen.

Benediction of the Perfumes:

The God of Abraham, the God of Isaac, the God of Jacob, bless here the creatures of these kinds that they may give forth the power of their odours so that neither the Enemy nor any false Imaginations may be able to enter into them, through our Lord Jesus Christ, to whom be honour and Glory now, henceforth, and for ever. Amen.

Sprinkle them with Holy Water, saying, Asperges me, Domine, etc.

Exorcism of Fire:

I exorcise thee, O thou creature of Fire, by Him by Whom all things are made, that forthwith thou wilt cast away every phantasm from thee that it shall not be able to do any hurt in any thing. Bless, O Lord, this creature of Fire and sanctify it, that it may be blessed to set forth the praise of Thy Holy Name that no hurt may be able to come unto me, through the virtue and defence of our Lord Jesus Christ. Amen.

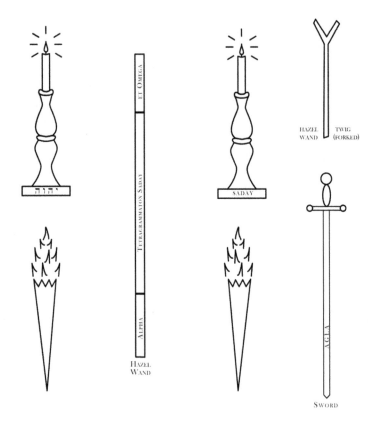

(Note on the reverse of the sword blade this Name: ON)

Invocations for the Days of the Week

Invocation for Sunday (SOL):
Come, Heavenly Spirits who have the effulgent rays of the Sun, Luminous Spirits who are ready to obey the power of the great Tetragrammaton, come and assist me in the operation that I am making under the auspices of the Grand Light of Day which the Eternal Creator hath formed for the use of universal nature. I invoke you for these purposes. Be favourable and auspicious to what I shall ask in the Name of Amioram, Adonai, Sabaoth.

Invocation for Monday (MOON):
Haste ye Sublime and Intelligent Genii who are obedient to the Sovereign Arcana, come and assist me in the operation that I undertake under the auspices of the Grand Luminary of the Night. I invoke you to this end and implore you to be favourable and hear my entreaties in the Name of Him Who commands the spirits who are Superiors in the regions that you inhabit. Bileth, Mizabu, Abinzaba.

Invocation for Tuesday (MARS):
Come Children of the Red Genii who have executed the order of the Sovereign Master of the Universe upon the armies of the rash Sennacherib, come and assist me in the operation that I undertake under the auspices of the third brilliant luminary of the firmament; be favourable to my entreaties in the Name of Adonay Sabaoth.

Invocation of Wednesday (MERCURY):

Run to me with speed, come to me ye Spirits of Mercury who preside over the operation of this day, hear favourably the present invocation that I make to you under the Divine Names of Venoel, Uranel, be kind and ready to second my undertakings. Render them efficacious.

Invocation for Thursday (JUPITER):

Come speedily ye blessed Spirits who preside over the operation of this day. Come, Incomprehensible Zebarel and all your legions, hasten to my assistance and be propitious to my undertakings, be kind and refuse me not your powerful aid and assistance.

Invocation for Friday (VENUS):

Come on the wings of the wind, ye happy Genii who preside over the workings of the heart. Come in the Name of the Great Tetragrammaton; hear favourably the Invocation that I make this day, destined to the wonder of love. Be ready to lend me your assistance to succeed in what I have undertaken under the hope that you will be favourable to me.

Invocation for Saturday (SATURN):

Come out of your gloomy solitude ye Saturnine spirits, come with your cohort, come with diligence to the place where I am going to begin my operation under your auspices; be attentive to my labours and contribute your assistance that it may resound to the honour and glory of the Highest.

They are called *Olympick* spirits, which do inhabit in the firmament, and in the stars of the firmament: and the office of these spirits is to declare Destinies, and to administer fatal Charms, so far forth as God pleaseth to permit them: for nothing, neither evil spirit nor evil Destiny, shall be able to hurt him who hath the most High for his refuge. If therefore any of the *Olympick* spirits shall teach or declare that which his star to which he is appointed portendeth, nevertheless he can bring forth nothing into action, unless he be permitted by the Divine power. It is God alone who giveth them power to effect it. Unto God the maker of all things, are obedient all things celestial, sublunary, and infernal. Therefore rest in this: Let God be thy guide in all things which thou undertakest, and all things shall attain to a happie and desired end; even as the history of the whole world testifieth and daily experience sheweth. There is peace to the godly: *there is no peace to the wicked, saith the Lord.*

There are seven different governments of the Spirits of *Olympus*, by whom God hath appointed the whole frame and universe of this world to be governed: and their visible stars are Aratron, Bethor, Phaleg, Och, Hagith, Ophiel, Phul, after the *Olympick* speech. Every one of these hath under him a mighty *Militia* in the firmament.

ARATRON ruleth visible Provinces XLIX.
BETHOR, XLII.
PHALEG, XXXV.
OCH, XXVIII.
HAGITH, XXI.
OPHIEL, XIIII.
PHUL, VII.

So that there are 182 *Olympick* Provinces in the whole Universe. wherein the seven Governours do exercise their power: all which are elegantly set forth in Astronomy. But in this place it is to be explained, in what manner these Princes and Powers may be drawn into communication. *Aratron* appeareth in the first hour of *Saturday*, and very truely giveth answers concerning his Provinces and Provincials. So likewise do the rest appear in order in their days and hours. Also, every one of them ruleth 490 years. The beginning of their simple order of years, in the 60th year before the Nativity of Christ, was the beginning of the administration of *Bethor*, and it lasted until the year of our Lord Christ 430. To whom succeeded *Phaleg*, until the 920th year. Then began *Och*, and continued until the year 1410, and thenceforth *Hagith* ruleth untill the year 1900.

Magically the Princes of the seven Governments are called simply, in that time, day and hour wherein they rule visibly or invisibly, by their Names and Offices which God hath given unto them; and by presenting their Character which they have given or confirmed.

The governor ***Aratron*** hath in his power those things which he doth naturally, that is, after the same manner and subject as those things which in Astronomy are ascribed to the power of *Saturn*.

Those things which he doth of his own free will, are,

1. That he can convert any thing into a stone in a moment, either animal or plant, retaining the same object to the sight.

2. He converteth treasures into coals, and coals into treasure.

3. He giveth familiars with a definite power.

4. He teacheth Alchymy, Magick, and Physick.

5. He reconcileth the subterranean spirits to men; maketh hairy men.

6. He causeth one to be invisible.

7. The barren he maketh fruitful, and giveth long life.

He hath under him 49 Kings, 42 Princes, 35 Presidents, 28 Dukes, 21 Ministers, standing before him; 14 familiars, seven messengers: he commandeth 36000 legions of spirits; the number of a legion is 490.

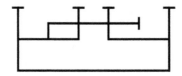

His Perfumes:

Black poppy seeds, henbane seed and mandrake root, lodestone powder and myrrh, mixed with the blood of a bat and the brain of a black cat. Form these into little pills and when dried use three by three as needed.

Heptameron: Sulphur

Recommended: Myrrh

Bethor governeth those things which are ascribed to Jupiter: he soon cometh being called. He that is dignified with his character, he raiseth to very great dignities, to cast open treasures: he reconcileth the spirits of the aire, that they give true answers: they transport precious stones from place to place, and they make medicines to work miraculously in their effects: he giveth also familiars of the firmament, and prolongeth life to 700 years if God will.

He hath under him 42 Kings, 35 Princes, 28 Dukes, 21 Counsellors, 14 Ministers, 7 Messengers, 29000 legions of Spirits.

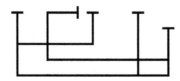

Perfumes:

Ash tree seeds, lignum aloes, storax, benzoin, ground lapis lazuli, Made into a paste with tops of peacock feathers, stork and swallow's blood and the brain of a hart.

Heptameron: Saffron

Recommended: Cedar

Phaleg ruleth those things which are attributed to Mars, the Prince of peace. He that hath his character he raiseth to great honours in warlike affaires.

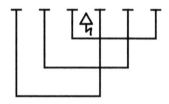

Perfumes:
Euphorbium, Bdellium, gum ammoniac, roots of both hellebores, powdered lodestone, and a touch of flowers of sulphur, mix well with the brain of a hart, the blood of a man and a black cat with the brain of a raven.
Heptameron: Pepper
Recommended: Dragon's Blood

Och governeth solar things; he giveth 600 years, with perfect health; he bestoweth great wisdom, giveth the most excellent Spirits, teacheth perfect Medicines: he converteth all things into most pure gold and precious stones: he giveth gold, and a purse springing with gold. He that is dignified with his Character, he maketh him to be worshipped as a Deity, by the Kings of the whole world.

He hath under him 36536 Legions: he administreth all things alone: and all his spirits serve him by centuries.

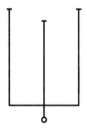

Perfumes:

Saffron, ambergris, musk, lignum aloes, fruit of laurel, cloves, myrrh, frankincense, a grain each of ambergris and musk, mixed with the brain of an eagle and blood from a white cock.

Heptameron: Red Wheat

Recommended: Frankincense

Hagith governeth Venereous things. He that is dignified with his Character, he maketh very fair, and to be adorned with all beauty. He converteth copper into gold, in a moment, and gold into copper: he giveth Spirits which do faithfully serve those to whom they are addicted.

He hath 4000 Legions of Spirits and over every thousand he ordaineth Kings for their appointed seasons.

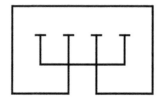

Perfumes:

Musk, ambergris, lignum aloes, red roses and powdered red coral, made into a paste with the blood of a dove or pigeon and sparrow's brain.

Heptameron: Pepperwort

Recommended: Red Sandalwood or Benzoin

Ophiel is the governour of such things as are attributed to Mercury: his Character is this.

His Spirits are 100000 Legions: he easily giveth Familiar Spirits: he teacheth all Arts: and he that is dignified with his Character, he maketh him to be able in a moment to convert Quicksilver into the Philosophers stone.

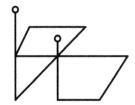

Perfumes:
Mastic, frankincense, cloves, cinquefoil, powdered agate, mixed with the brain of a fox and a weasel, and the blood of a magpie.
Heptameron: Mastick
Recommended: White Sandalwood

Phul hath chosen this character:

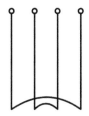

He changeth all metals into silver, in word and deed; governeth Lunary things; healeth the dropsie: he giveth spirits of the water, who do serve men in a corporeal and visible form; and maketh men to live 300 years.
Perfumes:
Frogs heads made of air and gathered after rain showers [common toad-stools?], eyes of a bull, seed of white poppy, camphor and frankincense, mixed with menstruous blood and the blood of a white gander.
Heptameron: Aloes
Recommended: Camphor or Jasmine

The most general Precepts of this Secret

1. Every Governour acteth with all his Spirits, either naturally, to wit, always after the same manner; or otherwise of their own free-will, if God hinder them not.

2. Every Governour is able to do all things which are done naturally in a long time, out of matter before prepared; and also to do them suddenly, out of matter not before prepared. As Och, the Prince of Solar things, prepareth gold in the mountains in a long time; in a less time, by the Chymical Art; and Magically, in a moment.

3. The true and divine Magician may use all the creatures of God, and offices of the Governours of the world, at his own will, for that the Governours of the world are obedient unto them, and come when they are called, and do execute their commands: but God is the Author thereof: as *Joshua* caused the Sun to stand still in heaven.

They send some of their Spirits to the mean Magicians, which do obey them only in some determinate business: but they hear not the false Magicians, but expose them to the deceits of the devils, and cast them into divers dangers, by the Command of God; as the Prophet *Jeremiah* testifieth, in his eighth Chapter, concerning the Jews.

4. In all the elements there are the seven Governours with their hosts, who do move with the equal motion of the firmament; and the inferiours do always depend upon the superiours, as it is taught in Philosophy.

5. A man that is a true Magician, is brought forth a Magician from his mother's womb: others, who do give themselves to this office, are unhappie. This is that which *John* the Baptist speaketh of: *No man can do any thing of himself, except it be given him from above.*

6. Every Character given from a Spirit, for what cause soever, hath his efficacie in this business, for which it is given, in the time prefixed: But it is to be used the same day and Planetary hour wherein it is given.

7. God liveth, and thy soul liveth: keep thy Covenant, and thou hast whatsoever the spirit shall reveal unto thee in God, because all things shall be done which the Spirit promiseth unto thee.

Aphorism 18

There are other names of the *Olympick* spirits delivered by others; but they only are effectual, which are delivered to any one, by the Spirit the revealer, visible or invisible: and they are delivered to every one as they are predestinated: therefore they are called Constellations; and they seldome have any efficacie above 40 years. Therefore it is most safe for the young practisers of Art, that they work by the offices of the Spirits alone, without their names; and if they are pre-ordained to attain the Art of Magick, the other parts of the Art will offer themselves unto them of their own accord. Pray therefore for a constant faith, and God will bring to pass all things in due season.

Aphorism 20

All things are possible to them that believe them, and are willing to receive them; but to the incredulous and unwilling, all things are impossible: there is no greater hinderance than a wavering minde, levity, inconstancy, foolish babbling, drunkenness, lusts, and disobedience to the word of God. A Magician therefore ought to be a man that is godly, honest, constant in his words and deeds, having a firm faith toward God, prudent, and covetous of nothing but of wisdom about divine things.

When you would call any of the *Olympick* Spirits, observe the rising of the Sun that day, and of what nature the Spirit is which you desire; and saying the prayer following, your desires shall he perfected:

Omnipotent and eternal God, who hast ordained the whole creation for thy praise and glory, and for the salvation of man, I beseech thee that thou wouldst send thy Spirit N.N. of the solar [or other] order, who shall inform and teach me those things which I shall ask of him; or, that he may bring me medicine against the dropsie, &c. Nevertheless, not my will be done, but thine, through Jesus Christ thy only begotten Son, our Lord. Amen.

But thou shalt not detain the Spirit above a full hour, unless he be familiarly addicted unto thee.

The License to depart:

Forasmuch as thou camest in peace, and quietly, and hast answered unto my petitions; I give thanks unto God, in whose Name thou camest: and now thou mayest depart in peace unto thy orders; and return to me again when I shall call thee by thy name, or by thy order, or by thy office, which is granted from the Creator. Amen.

Ecclesiastes. Chap. 5: Be not rash with thy mouth, neither let thy heart be hasty to utter any thing before God; for God is in Heaven, and thou in earth: Therefore let thy words be few; for a dream cometh through the multitude of business.

Book One: Part Two

CONTAINING Invocations, Conjurations, and Exorcisms; of the Bond of Spirits

Form of Conjuring and Exorcising Spirits to Appear

Oration to be said when putting on the Vestures: Amacor, Amacor, Amides, Theodomai, Aintor, by the merits of Thy Angels, O Lord, I will put on the garments of Righteousness, that this which I desire I may bring to perfection through the most holy Adonay, Whose kingdom endureth for ever and ever. Amen.

This on the other side:

The Lamen

Prayer

O Holy, Holy Lord God, from Whom all holy desires do proceed, I beg Thou wilt be merciful unto me at this time, granting I may become a True Magician and contemplate of Thy wondrous works at all times, in the Name of the Father and of the Son. Therefore in all my doings and at all times I will call upon Thy Most Holy Name, O Lord, for Thy help and assistance.

I beseech Thee, O Lord, that Thou wilt purge me and wash me in the blood of our Saviour, from all my sins and frailties, and that Thou wilt henceforward vouchsafe to keep and defend me from pride, lusts, cursing, blasphemy, unfaithfulness, and all other deadly sins and enormous offences, profaneness and spiritual wickedness; but that I may lead a godly, sober, faithful constant and pure life, walking uprightly in Thy sight, through the merits of Jesus Christ, Thy Son, our Lord and Saviour.

Omnipotent and Eternal Lord God Who sittest in Heaven and dost from thence behold all the dwellers upon earth, most mercifully I beseech Thee to hear and answer the petition of Thine unworthy servant, which I shall make unto Thee at this time, through Jesus Christ our Lord, Who liveth and reigneth with Thee in the unity of Thy Holy Spirit, ever One God, world without end.

Send down, O Lord, the Spirit of Thy Grace upon me. O God, put fear far from me, and give me an abundance in Thy faith, whereby all things are made possible unto man; put every wicked phantom far from my mind, and grant me true zeal, fervour, and intensive spirit of zeal, and prayer, that I may offer up a well-pleasing sacrifice unto Thee. Let me use Thy ministering spirits and Angels, O Lord, as thereby I may attain true wisdom and knowledge.

Our Father, etc.

Credo, etc.

Ave Maria, etc.

Glory be to the Father, Son, and Holy Ghost; as it was in the beginning, is now, and ever shall be, world without end. Amen.

Holy, Holy, Holy, Lord God of Sabaoth, which will come to judge the quick and the dead; Thou art Alpha and Omega, the first and the last, King of Kings, and Lord of Lords, Ioth, Abiel, Anathiel, Amasim, Alganabro, El, Sedomel, Gayes, Heli, Messias, Tolosm, Elias, Eschiros, Athanatos; by these Thy Holy Names, and all others, I do call upon Thee and beseech Thee, O Lord, by Thy Nativity and baptism, by Thy Cross and Passion, by Thine ascension, and by the coming of Thy Holy Ghost, by the bitterness of Thy Soul when it departed from Thy body; by Thine Angels, Archangels, prophets, patriarchs, and by all Thy Saints, and by all the Sacraments which are made in Thine honour, I do worship and beseech Thee, I bless and desire Thee, to accept these prayers and conjurations.

I implore Thee, O Holy Adonay, Amay, Horta, Vegadoro, Ysion, Ysesy, and by all Thy Holy Names, and by all Thine Angels, Archangels, and Powers, Dominations, and Virtues, and by Thy

Name with which King Solomon did bind up the devils and shut them up, Ethrack, Evanher, Agla, Goth, Joth, Othie, Venock, Nabrat, and by all Thy Holy Names which are written in this book, and by the virtue of them all, that Thou enable me to congregate all Thy spirits, that they may give me true answers to all my demands.

O Great and Eternal Virtue of the Highest, which Thou disposest their being come to judgment, Viachem, Stimilomaton, Esphares, Tetragrammaton, Oboram, Cryon, Elijtion, Onela, Brassim, Aoym, Messias, Soter, Emanuel, Sabaoth, Adonay, I worship Thee. I implore Thee with all the strength of my mind that by Thee my present prayers, consecrations, and conjurations may be hallowed. In the Name of the most merciful God of Heaven and of Earth, of the Seas and of the Infernals, by Thine Omnipotent help may I perform this Work.

Helie, Helion, Esseju, Deus Eternis, Eloy, Clemens Deus, Sanctus Sabaoth, Deus Exercillum, Adonay, Deus Mirabilis, Jao, Verax, Ampheneton, Saday, Dominator, On, Fortissimus Deus, invest with Thy blessed help this Work begun of Thee, that it may be consummated by Thy mighty power. Amen.

Amoruli, Tametia, Latisten, Rabur, Tanetia, Latisten, Escha, Aloelin, Alpha et Omega, Leytse, Oraston, Adonay. Amen.

Names and Offices of the Spirits. Messengers. and Intelligences of the Seven Planets

Presiding Spirits of Jupiter.	Presiding Spirits of Venus.	Presiding Spirits of Mars.	Presiding Spirits of Mercury.
Sachiel	Anael	Samael	Raphael
Castiel	Rachiel	Satael	Uriel
Asasiel	Sachiel	Amabiel	Seraphiel

Spirits of the Sun.
Gabriel
Vianathraba
Corat

Messengers of the Sun.
Burchat
Suceratos
Capabile

Intelligences of the Sun.
Haludiel
Machasiel
Chassiel

Spirits of the Moon.
Gabriel
Gabrael
Madios

Messengers of the Moon.
Anael
Pabael
Ustael

Intelligences of the Moon.
Uriel
Naromiel
Abuori

Spirits of Saturn.
Samael
Bachiel
Astel

Messengers of Saturn.
Sachiel
Zoniel
Hubaril

Intelligences of Saturn.
Mael
Orael
Valnum

Spirits of Jupiter.
Setchiel
Chedusitaniel
Corael

Messengers of Jupiter.
Turiel [See *Secret*
Grimoire of Turiel]
Coniel
Babiel

Intelligences of Jupiter.
Kadiel
Maltiel
Huphatriel
Estael

Spirits of Venus.
Thamael
Tenariel
Arragon

Messengers of Venus.
Colzras
Penjel
Penael

Intelligences of Venus.
Penat
Thiel
Rael
Teriapel

Spirits of Mercury.
Mathlai
Tarmiel
Baraborat

Messengers of Mercury.
Raphael
Ramel
Doremiel

Intelligences of Mercury.
Aiediat
Modiat
Sugmonos
Sallales

O Angeli Glorioso supradicti estote coadjutores et auxiliatores in omnibus negotijs et interrogationibus in omnibus caelestis causis per Eum qui venturus est judiciase vivos et mortuos.

Omnipotent and Eternal God Who hast ordained the whole creation for Thy praise and glory and for the salvation of man, I earnestly beseech Thee that Thou wouldst send one of Thy spirits of the Order of Jupiter, one of the messengers of Sachiel [or, in Olympic terms, Bethor] whom Thou hast appointed presiding spirit of Thy firmament at this time, most faithfully, willingly to show unto me those things which I shall demand or require of him, and truly execute my desires. Nevertheless, O most Holy God, Thy will and not mine be done, through Jesus Christ our Lord. Amen.

Invocation: I call upon thee, Sachiel, Castiel, and Asasiel, in the Name of the Father, and of the Son, and of the Holy Ghost, Blessed Trinity, Inseparable Unity, I invoke and entreat thee, Sachiel, Castiel, and Asasiel, in this hour to attend to the words and conjurations which I shall use by the Holy Names of God, El, Elohim, Elohe, Eeoba, Sabaoth, Elion, Eschiros, Adonay, Jay, Tetragrammaton, Saday; I conjure and excite you by the Holy Names of God, Hagios, Otheos, Ischyros, Athanatos, Paracletos, Agla, On, Alpha and Omega, Ausias, Tolimi, Elias, Imos, Amay, Horta, Vegadora, Antir, Sibranat, Amatha, Baldachia, Anuoram, Anexpheton, Via, Vita, Manus, Fons, Origo, Filius

and by all the other Holy, Glorious, Great, and Unspeakable, Mysterious, Mighty, Powerful, and Incomprehensible Names of God, that you attend unto the words which I shall utter, and send unto me Turiel, Coniel, or Babiel, messengers of your sphere, to tell unto me such things as I shall demand of him, in the Name of the Father, Son, and Holy Ghost.

I entreat thee, Setchiel, Chedustaniel, and Corael, by the whole host of Heaven, Seraphims, Cherubims, Thrones, Dominations, Virtues, Powers, Principalities, Archangels and Angels, by the great and glorious Spirits Orphaniel, Tetra, Pagiel, Salmia, Pastor, Salun, Azimor, and by your Star which is Jupiter, and by all the constellations of Heaven, and by whatsoever you obey, and by your Character which you have given and proposed and confirmed, that you attend unto me according to the prayers and petitions which I have made unto Almighty God, and that you forthwith send unto me one of your messengers who may willingly and truly and faithfully fulfil all my desires, wishes and commands, and that you command him to appear unto me in form of a beautiful angel clothed in white vestures, gently, courteously, kindly, and affably entering into communication with me, and that he neither bring terror nor fear unto me, or obstinately deny my requests, neither permitting any evil spirits to appear or approach in any way to hurt, terrify, or affright me, nor deceiving me in any wise; through the virtue of our Lord and Saviour Jesus Christ, in Whose Name I attend, waiting for and expecting your appearance. Fiat, Fiat, Fiat. Amen.

Interrogations
'Comest thou in peace, in the Name of the Father, and of the Son, and of the Holy Ghost?'
'Yes.'
'Thou art welcome, noble Spirit. What is thy name?'
'Turiel.'

'I have called thee here, Turiel, in the Name of Jesus of Nazareth, at Whose Name every knee doth bow, both of things in Heaven, Earth, and Hell, and every tongue shall confess there is no Name like unto the Name of Jesus, Who hath given power unto man to bind and to loose all things in His Name, yea, even unto them that trust in His salvation. Art thou the messenger of Setchiel?'

'Yes.'

'Wilt thou confirm thyself unto me at this time, and from henceforward reveal all things unto me that I shall desire to know and teach me how to increase my wisdom and knowledge, and show unto me the secrets of the Magick Art, and of the liberal sciences, that I may set forth the praise and glory of Almighty God?'

'Yes.'

'Then, I pray thee, give and confirm thy Character unto me, whereby I may call thee at all times, and also swear unto me this Oath, and I will righteously keep my vow and covenant unto Almighty God, and will courteously receive thee at all times when thou dost appear to me.'

Licence to Depart

Forasmuch as thou camest in peace and quietness and hast answered me and unto my petitions, I give humble and hearty thanks unto Almighty God, in whose Name I called thee and thou camest. And now thou mayest depart in peace unto thy Orders, and return unto me again at what time soever I shall call thee by thine own Oath, or by thy name, or by thine Order, or by thine Office which is granted from the Creator. And the Grace of God be with thee and me and upon the whole Israel of God. Amen. Glory be to the Father, and to the Son, and to the Holy Ghost, as it was in the beginning, is now, and ever shall be, world without end. Fiat. Fiat. Fiat. Amen.

Form of a Bond of Spirits given by Turiel, Messenger of the Spirits of Jupiter

Gloria Deo in Excelsis.

I, Turiel, Messenger of the Spirits of Jupiter, appointed thereunto by the Creator of all things visible and invisible, do swear and promise, and plighting faith and troth unto thee in the presence, by, and before the Great Lord of Heaven and the whole company of Heaven, by all the Holy Names of God, do swear and bind myself unto thee, by all the contents of God's Sacred Writ, by the Incarnation, death and passion, resurrection, and glorious Ascension of Jesus Christ, by all the Holy Sacraments, by the Mercy of God, by the Glory and Eyes of Heaven, by the forgiveness of sin, and hope of eternal salvation, by the Great Day of Doom, by all the Angels and Archangels, Seraphim, Cherubim, Dominations, Thrones, Principalities, Powers, and Virtues, Patriarchs, Prophets, Saints, Martyrs, Innocents, and all others of the blessed and glorious Company of Heaven, and by al! the sacred powers and virtues above rehearsed, and by whatever is holy and binding, thus do I swear now, and promise unto thee that I will hasten unto thee, and appear clearly unto thee at all times and places, and in all hours, days, and minutes, from this time forward until thy life's end, whensoever thou shalt call me by my name, or by my Office, and will come unto thee in what form thou shalt desire, whether it be visibly or invisibly; I will answer all thy desires. And in testimony whereof, and before all the Powers of Heaven, I have hereunto set, subscribed, and confirmed my Character unto thee.

So help me God. Fiat. Amen.

FINIS

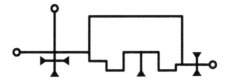

BOOK TWO: PLANETARY DAYS AND HOURS

TIMING OF OPERATIONS

In general, grimoire magic requires all activity to take place under a waxing Moon, and preferably as soon after the New Moon as possible. In addition, it requires planetary days and hours to be used – the operator is advised to learn how to calculate these. The days and hours of Mercury are chiefly employed in making the tools, with some exceptions. The first hour of each planetary day is also the hour of that planet, so Dawn operations are at least implied. There are several traditional sources that recommend Dawn for the cutting of wands as well as for magical operations or meditations, so we may infer that the first hour of the day is preferred except when we are buying our materials, when a later hour of the planet will suit our purpose

THE PLANETARY DAYS

Hopefully, all are aware that in traditional sources the Sun rules Sunday, the Moon Monday, Mars Tuesday, Mercury Wednesday, Jupiter Thursday, Venus Friday and Saturn Saturday. These names of the days are derived from names of Norse gods plus Sun, Moon and Saturn. The attribution of the planets to the days is encountered in the Greco-Egyptian papyri (where Saturday becomes 'Kronos', and so for the rest) as well as the much later grimoires, and is likely of 'Chaldean' origin, as is the seven-day week. The planetary hours schema is also encountered at around the same time and the two are in fact mathematically inseparable.

That is, if we allocate the hours of the day to the seven planets in a regular cycle, commencing with the planet whose day it is, then the next day will start with the hour of the planet ruling it, and so on continuously. This pattern evidently depends on a close relationship between seven and twelve. At this stage it should be pointed out that the traditional planetary hours are not the same as our one o'clock, two o'clock, although there are still twelve of them to each day, and another twelve for the night.

The Planetary Hours of the Day are calculated by finding the number of minutes between Sunrise and Sunset and dividing by twelve; thus the first hour begins at local sunrise and consists of one twelfth of real daytime. The same process is then applied to the time between local Sunset and Sunrise, to obtain the Planetary Hours of the Night.

Since Saturday illustrates the pattern best, we shall use the Day of Saturn as our example. Sunrise on Saturday begins the hour of Saturn, followed by the hour of Jupiter, then that of Mars, Sun, Venus, Mercury and the Moon, the eighth hour being again that of Saturn, with Jupiter, Mars, Sun, Venus ruling the remaining hours. Sunset on Saturday makes no change to the cycle, being ruled by

Mercury, and so the cycle continues through the night, until Sunrise on Sunday begins with the hour of the Sun.

The first hour of each day therefore is ruled by the same planet as the day itself. Very often in the grimoires we are told to do such and such in the day and hour of Mercury (for example). This frequently means Sunrise, which saves a lot of calculation. It also gives us the energy of the day at source (and when the Sun is on the Ascendant, the Moon is automatically conjunct the Part of Fortune). However, it does not *always* mean Sunrise; if for example we are told to buy such and such in the day and hour of Mercury, we'll be hard put to find a store open at Dawn, so very likely the Eighth planetary hour is intended.

There may or may not be a measurable relationship between the planets and the days and hours to which they are attributed. What there is however is a clear relationship between the evolution of the week and the lunar month of 28 days, with the Sabbaths once marking the four quarter days of a lunation. The magician, seeking to make reality malleable via his symbols, has much to gain from the Days and Hours of the Planets. Thus, we tap into rhythms that reverberate through our entire culture, and impose a rhythm on our magical activities that increases our momentum and enriches and deepens the fabric of our experiences.

While dealing with matters beyond 'grimoire primer' level, the following elaboration, excerpted from my *Testament of Cyprian the Mage*, is a necessary and helpful digression. It is not infrequently argued against the planetary hours that they bear no observable connection with the planets of Astrology. The reason for this is quite simple: they are not meant to. What there is however is a clear relationship historically with another astrological feature altogether, the Egyptian decans. Hellenistic and later astrology imposed a planetary attribution on these which has helped obscure the relationship – among the most solid instances of a relationship between the magic of the *PGM* and earlier with the methodology of the grimoires.

Gods of Time

From *Testament of Cyprian the Mage*, Vol. 1

(London: Scarlet Imprint,2014) p. 160

It is well past time to acknowledge where began my interest in the decans and lunar mansions, and my appreciation of their importance in the history of magic. These themes, though long all but ignored by modern occultism, were enthusiastically researched by the Warburg Institute as being of immense cultural significance. It is still impossible to improve on the succinct comments of Frances Yates: 'Into the Hellenistic astrology which is the background of the philosophical *Hermetica* an Egyptian element had been absorbed, namely the thirty-six decans... [which] were really Egyptian sidereal gods of time who had become absorbed in the Chaldean astrology and affiliated to the zodiac.' Thus indeed the decans originate with the ancient Egyptians, whose year began with the heliacal rising of the star Sothis (Sirius) in Cancer. The corresponding decan was attributed to Sothis, who 'looked back' at the decans to come.

Simplistically speaking the decans would rise with the Sun for ten days each year until the reappearance of Sothis, the first and last. As this cycle continued and the decans progressed to the West they descended into the Underworld, not to reappear for 70 days. There is wide agreement that they are the origin of the 24-hour clock, as also of 'planetary' hours. At the time of the heliacal rising of Sothis in the summer, twelve decans rose before dawn. Ten hours of daylight, to which were added an hour of twilight at either end of the day, gave us the 24-hour clock.

Initially these hours were equal divisions of day and night. In time the 'equinoctial hours', when day and night are of equal length, were adopted as standard. This historical excursion is important to establish that the 'god of the hour', mentioned in various magical papyri, was intended to be the current decan lord rather than a planetary ruler. This is an indicator that the decans are of general rather than specialised significance in the evolution of grimoire magic.

From the time of the Middle Kingdom they appear frequently painted on coffin lids. Many lists of decans are known, involving considerable variation. In the New Kingdom royal tombs contained lists of the decans; this was extended to royal officials in the time of Rameses (1292–1075 BCE). In the tomb of Rameses VI (1145–1137 BCE) the decans are depicted worshipping the resurgent god of the Sun. Their reputation appears at first to have been wholly benign. Up to the Late Period they were depicted in temple and tomb art. Tombs of the 18th and 19th Dynasties have ceilings painted with the decans; elaborate versions in the tombs of Rameses IV and Seti I both portray their night journey, as for 70 days they travel through the underworld. The origins of their ambivalent reputation begin in the 21st Dynasty (1075–945 BCE), when some officials began to wear amulets protecting them from particular decans.

Initially independent of the zodiac, in the Ptolemaic era these decans were assimilated to the Greco-Babylonian system; they have been a feature of Western astrology ever since.

Egyptian and Hermetic Decans

From *Testament of Cyprian the Mage*, Vol. 1
(London: Scarlet Imprint,2014) p. 169

The decans were always called 'gods' by the
proponents of the Egyptian tradition. (*L'Astrologie
Grecque*, A. Bouche-Leclercq.)

The decan spirits began as gods. In the fusion of ideas in
antiquity, wherever Egyptian influence was strongest this
identity was retained. This included Hellenised astrologers
like Hephestion of Thebes whose astrology was transposed
from the Sothic to the Aries start point. Hephestion
(otherwise Hephaestion) was an astrological writer of
Egyptian descent in the early 5th century. His *Apotelesmatika*
involved sympathies with the more 'mythological astrology'
of Dorotheus of Sidon (1st century), among others, and a
wish to reintegrate it with the dominant 'rational astrology'
of Claudius Ptolemy (2nd century). He is an important
source as a compiler of the earlier strains of Hellenistic
astrology when the emergent synthesis underlying the
Western system was taking shape. The details he provides
of the decans in Greco-Egyptian astrology are among the
most authoritative we possess.

Elsewhere, under Chaldean or Jewish influence, the
decans developed or endured various other guises: syncretic
arrays of cosmopolitan deities; opposed gods in pairs; demons
with thwarting angels; demons pure and simple. In all these
forms, however, once absorbed into the astrologically based
synthesis of the Hellenistic world they exerted a powerful
and lasting influence. Their elastic hierarchical structures,
which are and always were self-contained pantheons, had a

powerful influence on all subsequent Western demonology in and out of the grimoires. The Egyptian influence upon words of power in magical texts consists of exactly such lists of nigh unintelligible names. The spirit images of the *Goetia of Solomon*, of surreal zoological forms, emerged with all their various characteristics from those of the mansions and decans. Equally the tabulated amuletic images, stones, herbs and animals, sympathetic and antipathetic, either originated or comprehended much traditional lore in their expansive embrace.

With so extensive a role it is important to understand from the outset the underlying principles, practical and theoretical. It must be borne in mind that the Egyptian decans were not originally similar to the Hellenistic conception. The number was not originally fixed at 36, and the decans were not of equal size; moreover, their names and order changed a good deal (*HWA* p.20). More importantly they originally evolved quite separately from the zodiac, nor were they confined to the ecliptic. Like the mansions they were originally wholly identified with stars and constellations. Even though connected with the Sun's rising in the East, they stretched even further from the ecliptic than do the lunar mansions, extending to the tropics. In the papyri and earlier they also had a relationship of some kind with the Polar constellations. Originally the term 'decan' was not a definition. The form 'bekan' is found in Egyptian, among other names; the resemblance to 'deka', meaning ten in Greek, is completely coincidental. Nevertheless, the importance of the numbers 10 and 36 in Pythagorean thought commended this division to the Greeks, while zodiacal and planetary concerns and attributions were imposed in line with the Chaldean system.

In accepting conventional astrological ideas into our modern handling of the decans – and indeed the mansions – it is necessary to emphasise certain provisos. Firstly, the conventions of Tropical Astrology employed do not cancel the importance of individual star positions and constellations, they only enable calculations in relation to them (outlining my objections to beginning with a Sidereal astrological system would require too much of a digression even by my standards). Secondly, distance from the ecliptic is largely irrelevant; any star – even Polaris – can be related to a degree of celestial longitude. Rheinhold Ebertin's existing work with the Fixed Stars has already introduced this concept to our era, contradictory though it is of conventional astrological dogma.

> Some fixed stars are of very great declination from the ecliptic. Some… are of the opinion that fixed stars with large declination, and if more than 23 degrees away from the celestial equator, are of no use in practical interpretation. Practice, however, does not bear out this opinion. Moreover, practice shows that this declination does not appear to matter at all. (*Fixed Stars & their Interpretation*, Ebertin-Hoffman.)

In this way both mansions and decans can retain their stellar character and observational importance within a Tropical schema. At the same time, in accord with astrological thinking and post-Sothic decans, the solsticial and equinoctial points are granted similar status to the important Fixed Stars and constellations.

Alternative Invocations: Sabean Planetary Magic

The planetary angels of the section following are evident equivalents of those in the grimoires. It also employs the so-called 'Chaldean order' of the planets reproduced in the various *Keys* of Solomon.

Planet	*Picatrix* angels	Grimoire angels
Saturn	Asbil	Cassiel
Jupiter	Rufijail	Tzadkiel
Mars	(Ru) Bijail	Samael
Sun	Ba'il	Mikael
Venus	Bitail	Aniel
Mercury	Harqil	Raphael
Moon	Saljail	Gabriel

Note that in this system, the Sun and Venus are associated with Ba'il, i.e. Baal, and Bitail, i.e. Baalit, (the feminine form, thus Lord and Lady). The association of Bael, the chief god, with the Sun has its equivalent in 'Orphic' solar theology. In the alternative system tabulated below, Bel or Marduk is associated with Jupiter, showing its roots in a schema more compatible with the Olympian or Jovist theology. Thus, the variant identifications of the Sun or Jupiter as chief deity, encountered in various Greek systems, both have analogues in the Middle East.

Planet	Day	Sabean Name	Babylonian Name	Greek Name
Sun	Sunday	Samas	Shamash	Helios
Moon	Monday	Sin	Sin	Selene
Mars	Tuesday	Nergal	Nergal	Ares
Mercury	Wednesday	Nabu	Nabu	Hermes
Jupiter	Thursday	Bel	Marduk	Zeus
Venus	Friday	Beltis	Ishtar	Aphrodite
Saturn	Saturday	Kronos	Ninib	Kronos

That these pagan gods are essentially equivalent to the 'angels' named in the Sabean rites we see from further incantations of theirs in the *Picatrix*. These, with other details omitted in the condensed form given here, give their names in various tongues, chiefly Arab, Persian, Roman (Eastern Empire, thus Greek in most cases), Greek and Indian. Despite some little confusion, these names are eminently recognisable in most cases. Still other Sabean incantations given in the same book omit the angel names altogether and simply use the Greek names; while the author says that when sacrificing a bull to Saturn, they repeat a prayer of the Greeks. The flexibility of astrological syncretism is visible in the second series of incantations: while using male names for the Sun they address her as the queen of heaven and the Moon as Lord.

For immediate purposes I recommend the sigils of the Olympic Spirits for the characters mentioned. Some students may prefer those from the *Picatrix* (see *Geosophia: The Argo of Magic*, Scarlet Imprint, 2010).

Sabean Rites of the Planets from the Picatrix

Saturn: first fast seven days from the day of the Sun till the day of Saturn, on the seventh day sacrifice a black raven (and a black dog as some say) saying over it:

'In the Names of Asbil who is set over Saturn, and of the Lords of the Highest Houses, attend to my commands and fulfil all I desire of thee.'

Then employ the character of Saturn to obtain what you will.

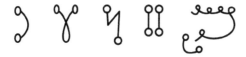

Jupiter: again fast, seven days from Friday to the day of Jupiter. On the seventh day sacrifice a black sheep and consume the liver, saying:

'O Rufijail, thou angel that is set over Jupiter, the happy, the good, the perfect beauty! By the Lords of the Highest Houses, hear and attend to my invocation and fulfil all I desire of thee.'

Then use the character of Jupiter to obtain thy desires.

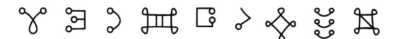

Mars: fasting seven days from the day of Mercury to the day of Mars, one sacrifices a wild, black cat, or as some say a spotted cat, consuming its liver and saying over it:

'O (Ru) Bijail, thou Angel who is set over Mars, the vehement, the ardent, the inflammatory horseman! By the Lords of the Highest Houses, attend to my demands!'

Then one may employ the character to obtain one's will.

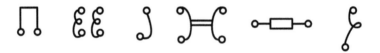

Sun: fast seven days from Monday to the day of the Sun, one sacrifices a calf, eating its liver, saying:

'O Ba'il, thou Angel that is set over the Sun, the bright, the world keeper, full light and perfect brilliance, the bringer of good and ill fortune, the helpful and harmful! By the Lords of the Highest Houses, attend and do my will!'

One may then use the character for one's purpose.

Venus: this operation requires a fast from Saturday unto the day of the planet. One sacrifices a white dove, consuming its liver, and sayeth:

'O Bitail, thou Angel that art set over Venus, the Fortunate, Beautiful Star! By the Lords of the Highest Houses, attend and do my will!'

Then use the character for one's purpose.

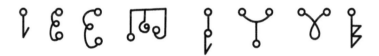

Mercury: for the operation of this planet one fasts from the day of Jupiter to that of Mercury, and on this day one must sacrifice a black and white cock, or as some say a black, green and white cock, eating its liver and saying:

'O Harqil, thou Angel who art set over Mercury, the fortunate, noble, beautifully formed one, by the Lords of the Highest Houses, attend and do my will.'

Then use his character for your purpose.

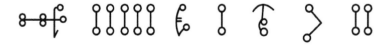

Moon: fast seven days from Tuesday until her day. On the seventh day slaughter a sheep and eat its liver saying:

'Saljail thou Angel who art set over the Moon, the key and the chief of stars, the light, the quick! By the Lords of the Highest Houses, attend and do my will!'

Then use the character to obtain what you will.

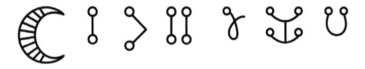

Saturn: 'In the name of God, in the name of the Angel Isbil, who is set over Saturn in all coldness and ice, the Lord of the Seventh Sphere, I invoke you by all your names: in Arabic, O Zuhal, in Persian, O Kewan, In Roman, O Kronos, in Greek, O Kronos, in Hindi, O Sanasara! By the Lord of the Highest House, may you grant my request, listen to my call, and obey me in obedience to God and his rulership, grant me NN.'

Jupiter: 'O Rufijail, you angel who are set over Jupiter, joyful and serene, complete, consummate, pious, Lord of beautiful vestments, of dignity and wisdom, far from that which is unclean and from vulgar speech! I invoke you by all your names: In Arabic, O Mustari, in Persian, O Birgis, In Iranian, O Hormuz [Ormazd], in Greek, O Zeus, in Hindi, O Wihasfati! By the Lord of the Highest House, of good deeds and of mercy, may you grant me NN.'

Mars: 'O Rubijail, you angel who are set over Mars, you violent, hard-headed, fiery, flaming, brave hearted, blood spiller, rouser of civil war and of the mob, powerful and virile, you who forceth, who overcometh, inconstant, violent, lord of ill deeds, punishment, blows, captivity, deceit, falsely accusing, speaker of uncouth words, pitiless, thou slayer, dwelling alone and apart, bearer of arms and prolific fornicator. I invoke you by all your names: In Arabic, O Mirrih, in Persian, O Bahram, In Roman, O Ares [Mars], in Greek, O Ares, in Hindi, O Angara! By the Lord of the Highest House, attend my word and grant my petition, for see I desire that you do NN by Rubijail, the angel set over your realm.'

At Dawn to the Sun: 'O Cause of Causes, you are sanctified and made sacred and ruleth unceasingly and forever, I petition you (insert here a petition for favour and recognition from a specified lord) or from all the kings of the earth. Welcome, thou who bringest forth the light and the life of the world, deign to listen to me and grant me recognition and kind reception. I invoke you by all your names: In Arabic, O Sams, in Persian, O Mihr (Mitra?), In Roman, O Helios, In Hindi, O Aras, O Bara! O light and radiance of the world, who art the centre of all, who giveth life to the world of coming forth and passing away, attending to its growth, o you who standeth in the exalted places, you who holds the supreme place (insert petition for favour), for you are mistress and queen [!] of the planets, they who receive and emit their light and radiance from you. I beseech thee, who guidest everything, take pity on me, my prayer and my petition.'

Venus: 'Hail unto thee, O Venus Anahid (Anahita), joyous mistress, the cool, the moist, constant, clean, beauteous, sweet-smelling, open handed, happy, mistress of ornament, of gold, of gaiety, of dance, of joyous arousal, of finery, of singing and of hearing songs, of flute playing, of beautiful music from plucking of strings, of recreation and jest of company and leisure, thou friendly and receptive, arouser of love, the just, thou who lovest wines, luxury, all joys and union. Thus art thou; I invoke you by all your names: In Arabic, O Zuhara, in Persian, O Anahid, in Roman, O Diana [of Ephesus], in Greek, O Aphrodite, in Hindi, O Surfa, O Astarte! By the Lord of the Highest House, may you hear me and fill us all with your love and the joy of your roving dance. By Bitail, the angel who is set over your realm, come fill us forever and ever again with the sweet breath of your life!'

When Mercury is conjunct the Moon: 'Hail unto thee, O Mercury, O Lord, excellent, trustworthy, replete with wisdom, speaker, comprehensible, who disputeth knowingly, aware of every science, thou that calculateth, scribe, of beautiful manners, who knoweth that happening in heaven and earth, thou lord, noble one, caring little for pleasure, that art useful to goods and in trading, lord of cunning, of deceit and cleverness, thou that aideth, patient, clever, deft handed, lord of revelation and of prophets, of the proof of the divine, of faith, of understanding, of speech, messages, sound teaching, of diverse arts, of perception, insight, sound knowledge, of philosophy, of foreknowledge, of the measuring of heaven and earth, of surveying, of astrology, of augury, of casting lots, of rhetoric, of skill in verse, of accounting, of eloquence, of sweet, swift flowing and elegant speech, of inscrutability, of rapidity in trade, of much travel, of deception, of elegance, of sureness, of assistance, of flexibility, of patience, of wishing good, of fairness, of mercy, of peace, of dignity, of self-control, of the right reverence of the divine, of recognition of rights and sweet spoken. Thou art concealed, so that no nature knoweth thee, and subtle, so that thou art not defined by any description; thus thou art a bringer of fortune with the fortunate stars, male with the male, female with the female, daily with diurnal stars, nightly with nocturnal stars, thou maketh thyself like unto them in nature and in all their actions. Thus art thou, I call you by all your names: In Arabic, O Utarid, in Persian, O Tir, In Iranian, O Haruz, in Greek, O Hermes, in Hindi, O Buddha! By the Lord of the Highest House and the supreme ruler, may you hear me and obey me in all I ask of thee... grant me NN by Harqil, the angel who is set over your realm, may you hear my prayer and attend my petition...'

Moon: 'Hail unto thee O Moon, O fortunate Lord, blessed, cool, moist, constant, beauteous, thou key and chief of stars, moving easily, wanderer, thou that possesseth the far reaching light, of the radiant shining, of joy, of praise and reward, thou fortunate lord, learned in religion, who deeply considereth all things, knowing, ruling subtly, who loveth music, jest and play, ruler of heralds, of messages, of the disclosing of secrets, giving, noble, mild, strong! Thou art the one whose sphere is nearest of all to us and most powerfully bring good and ill, thou art the one who makes bonds between the planets, transmitting their light and turneth to good that which favours us not; through your good will all becomes good, through your ill will all turneth to ill, thou art the first and last among all things, and to you belongeth rule and priority over all planets. Thus art thou, I ask thee, by Silijail, the angel who is set over your realm, deign to take pity on my lowly petition and prayer to you, and hearken obediently unto God and his authority, granting me what I beseech and desire of you. Behold, I invoke you by all your names: In Arabic, O Qamar, in Persian, O Mah, in Iranian, O Samail, in Roman, O Selene, in Hindi, O Soma! Hearken unto me'.

Hymns to the Planetary Gods

As further material for supplementation and adaptation, I present here hymns to the planetary gods from various sources, chiefly ancient. These may be used in various ways, for example as short invocations as discussed in the Sixfold Process of Evocation following, and in the consecration of talismans, as indeed of material spells in general.

ODE TO THE SUN

Latium invokes thee, Sol, because thou alone art in honour after the Father the centre of light, and they affirm that thy sacred head bears a golden brightness in twelve rays, because thou formest the numbers of the months and that number of hours. They say that thou guidest four winged steeds, because thou alone rulest the chariot of the elements. For dispelling darkness thou revealest the shining heavens. Hence they esteem thee Phoebus (Apollo), the discoverer of the secrets of the future, or because thou preventest nocturnal crimes. Egypt worships thee as Isoean Serapis, and Memphis as Osiris. Thou art worshipped by different rites as Mithra, Dis, and the cruel Typhon. Thou art also the beautiful Atys and the fostering son of the bent plough. Thou art the Ammon of barren Libya, and the Adonis of Byblos. Thus under varied appellations the whole world worships thee.

Hail, thou true image of the gods and of thy father's face, thou whose sacred name, surname, and omen, three letters make to agree with the number 608.

Martianus Capella, 4th Century CE

INVOCATION OF THE MOON GODDESS

I call upon you who have all forms and many names, Double-horned goddess, Mene. Whose form none knows save IAO alone, Creator of the Universe; Who shaped you into the 28 shapes of the world:

Thus do you complete every form and distribute breath to every living thing that it might flourish. Thou who waxest from obscurity into light, and diminisheth into darkness.

The first companion of your name is Silence,
The second a popping sound,
The third a low groaning,
The fourth a sustained hissing,
The fifth a cry of joy!
The sixth a moaning noise,
The seventh as the barking of dogs;
The eighth a mighty bellowing;
The ninth as the neighing of horses.
The tenth a musical sound,

The eleventh a sounding wind,
The twelfth a wind creating sound,
The thirteenth a sound of coercion:
The ultimate a coercive emanation from Perfection!

Ox, vulture, bull, beetle, falcon, crab, dog, Wolf, serpent,
horse, she-goat, asp, kid, he-goat, Baboon, cat, lion,
leopard, fieldmouse, deer, multiform, Virgin, torch,
lightning, garland, heralds wand, child, key!
    I have spoken your signs and the symbols of your
name that you might hear me, Mistress of the World,
Stable One, Mighty One!

                                          From PGM LXX. 4-25

MARS

The other gods are weaker; thou alone
Dost break the king and bend the emperor's knee:
Lower than unto Christ they bow to thee,
Lord of the slave, and guardian of the free,
Steel-hearted Ares, shaker of the throne.
Young god of battle, restless lover, hail!
For, once a man has seen thine eyes aflame,
And mounted on the horses of the gale,
Death is a nothing, life an empty name:
Arise and lead us ere our blood be tame.

From 'Ares: God of War' by Herbert Asquith, *The Volunteer
    and Other Poems*. London: Sidgwick & Jackson, 1917.

MERCURY

Come unto me, Lord Hermes, even as into women's wombs come babes!

Come unto me, Lord Hermes, who dost collect the food of gods and men!

Lord Hermes, come to me, and give me grace, food, victory, health, happiness, and cheerful countenance, beauty and powers in sight of all!

I know thy Name that shineth forth in heaven; I know thy forms as well;

I know thy tree; I know thy wood as well.

I know thee, Hermes, who thou art, and whence thou art, and what thy city is.

I know thy names in the Egyptian tongue, and thy true name as it is written on the holy tablet in the holy place at Hermes' city, where thou dost have thy birth.

I know thee, Hermes, and thou me; I am thou, and thou art I.

Come unto me; fulfil all that I crave; be favourable to me together with good fortune and the blessing of the Good.

(Hermes Hymn from the papyri, via GRS Mead)

JUPITER

Zeus was the first, Zeus last, the lightning's lord,
Zeus head, Zeus centre, all things are from Zeus.
Zeus born a male, Zeus virgin undefiled;
Zeus the firm base of earth and starry heaven;
Zeus sovereign, Zeus alone first cause of all:

One power divine, great ruler of the world,
One kingly form, encircling all things here,
Fire, water, earth, and ether, night and day;
Wisdom, first parent, and delightful Love:
For in Zeus' mighty body these all lie.
His head and beauteous face the radiant heaven
Reveals and round him float in shining waves
The golden tresses of the twinkling stars.
On either side bulls' horns of gold are seen,
Sunrise and sunset, footpaths of the gods.
His eyes the Sun, the Moon's responsive light;
His mind immortal ether, sovereign truth,
Hears and considers all; nor any speech,
Nor cry, nor noise, nor ominous voice escapes
The ear of Zeus, great Kronos' mightier son:
Such his immortal head, and such his thought.
His radiant body, boundless, undisturbed
In strength of mighty limbs was formed thus:
The god's broad-spreading shoulders, breast and back
Air's wide expanse displays, on either side
Grow wings, wherewith throughout all space he flies.
Earth the all-mother, with her lofty hills,
His sacred belly forms; the swelling flood
Of hoarse resounding Ocean girds his waist.
His feet the deeply rooted ground upholds,
And dismal Tartarus, and earth's utmost bounds.
All things he hides, then from his heart again
In godlike action brings to gladsome light.

(Orphic Fragment 3, from *Porphyry, On Cult Images - Fragments from Eusebius*, Praeparatio Evangelica (1903), Translated by Edwin Hamilton Gifford,)

VENUS

Heavenly, illustrious, laughter-loving queen,
Sea-born, night-loving, of an awful mien;
Crafty, from whom Necessity first came,
Producing, nightly, all-connecting dame:
'Tis thine the world with harmony to join,
 for all things spring from thee, O pow'r divine.
The triple Fates are rul'd by thy decree,
And all productions yield alike to thee:
Whate'er the heavens, encircling all contain,
Earth fruit-producing, and the stormy main,
Thy sway confesses, and obeys thy nod,
Awful attendant of the strongest God:
Goddess of marriage, charming to the sight,
Mother of Loves, whom banquetings delight;
Source of persuasion, secret, favouring queen,
Illustrious born, apparent and unseen:
Spousal, Lupercalian, to love inclined,
Prolific, most-desired, life-giving, kind:
Great sceptre-bearer of the Gods, 'tis thine,
Mortals in necessary bands to join.
And every tribe of savage monsters dire
In magic chains to bind, through mad desire.

From the *Orphic Hymns*, Thomas Taylor, 1792.

SATURN

Ethereal father, mighty Titan, hear,
Great fire of Gods and men, whom all revere:
Endued with various council, pure and strong,
To whom perfection and decrease belong.
Consumed by thee all forms that hourly die,
By thee restored, their former place supply;
The world immense in everlasting chains,
Strong and ineffable thy power contains
Father of vast eternity, divine,
O mighty Saturn, various speech is thine:
Blossom of earth and of the starry skies,
Husband of Rhea, and as Prometheus wise.

From the *Orphic Hymns*, Thomas Taylor, 1792.

The Hours of the Day

♄	☉	☽	♂	☿	♃	♀
♃	♀	♄	☉	☽	♂	☿
♂	☿	♃	♀	♄	☉	☽
☉	☽	♂	☿	♃	♀	♄
♀	♄	☉	☽	♂	☿	♃
☿	♃	♀	♄	☉	☽	♂
☽	♂	☿	♃	♀	♄	☉
♄	☉	☽	♂	☿	♃	♀
♃	♀	♄	☉	☽	♂	☿
♂	☿	♃	♀	♄	☉	☽
☉	☽	♂	☿	♃	♀	♄
♀	♄	☉	☽	♂	☿	♃

The Hours of the Night

☿	♃	♀	♄	☉	☽	♂
☽	♂	☿	♃	♀	♄	☉
♄	☉	☽	♂	☿	♃	♀
♃	♀	♄	☉	☽	♂	☿
♂	☿	♃	♀	♄	☉	☽
☉	☽	♂	☿	♃	♀	♄
♀	♄	☉	☽	♂	☿	♃
☿	♃	♀	♄	☉	☽	♂
☽	♂	☿	♃	♀	♄	☉
♄	☉	☽	♂	☿	♃	♀
♃	♀	♄	☉	☽	♂	☿
♂	☿	♃	♀	♄	☉	☽

APPENDIX I: THE SIXFOLD PROCESS OF EVOCATION: CLASSICAL AND MODERN

Two Ritual Frames

In this section two ritual structures will be discussed on very conventional lines; these are essentially 'frames', whereby an existing ritual can be analysed in terms of identifiable components, or an original one composed. In the former case, fragments of ritual, or isolated components in textual sources, may be identified through knowledge of these frames, and reconstructions undertaken. In the latter, collating existing components, or undertaking composition of rituals from scratch, are clearly facilitated in much the same way. In practice, both situations may apply, more often than not.

The Grimoire Frame

Stephen Skinner and others have hypothesised (I do not say proven) that a 'classical' conjuration ritual consists of six stages. The reader is encouraged to consult his *Goetia of Doctor Rudd* (p.91 onwards). Traditional or otherwise, the procedure certainly possesses qualities worth consideration. For our purposes it is better to examine various rites from this perspective, rather than take the *Goetia* as setting a standard. These stages, give or take some variation, are as follows:

Consecratio Dei

Literally, 'the dedication to God'. Skinner interprets this as preliminary prayers, seeking, essentially, to link oneself to God as a first line of defence against the spirits. His mention of John Dee's tedious prayers before Angelic conversations are not terribly apropos; Dee shunned the grimoires, and his pious adaptations are not necessarily analogous. More usefully, he cites the widespread use of the Seven Penitential Prayers by grimoire magicians in this capacity. Thus, we can readily identify this stage in the ritual process of the *True Grimoire*, for example, as part of the preparation of the Circle in the initial ceremonies to be precise.

Given this, it may be useful to give *Consecratio Dei* a more nuanced translation of 'Divine Consecration'. Essentially it encapsulates the initial stages of the modern ritual structure to be examined further on. That is, the Divine Consecration could be broken down into banishings (including invocation of guardians); purifications with holy water; consecrations with incense or Holy Oil; and finally, the Oath, particularly stressing its Confessional aspect. Alternatively, these facets might be combined into a single preliminary rite: banishings through to consecrations, leading into the Confession (as in *Liber Pyramidos*). As will be detailed anon, this single stage essentially contains the three first stages of the modern ceremonial approach. Such a unified structure – shorn of pentagrams and other novelties – is worthy of emulation. An excellent modern example is the Opening by *Pyramidos*.

Invocatio

Here too, the commentary on the modern equivalent essentially applies, particularly the necessity of a 'Preliminary Invocation', specifically of an intermediary spirit. This is the only element either understated or missing from Crowley's or Skinner's analyses respectively.

Constrictio

Otherwise called the *Reception of the Spirit*. While the sense of Binding is important to recognise, the much-vaunted Triangle of Art need not be involved here for this to be relevant. It is simply the right time for testing that the spirit is who it says it is; also, as the alternative title implies, for greeting it while assessing the situation and assuring yourself of the spirit's willingness to acquiesce to your designs. The subtle student will perceive an opportunity, for instance of greeting the spirit in the names of the superiors already invoked. Different forms, but with identical intentions, are to be found in the Faustian grimoires and elsewhere.

Ligatio

This is, as Skinner notes, the binding of the spirit with an oath. The word 'conjure' means to swear together, so this is clearly the most important aspect of the ritual – its central intention. Clearly – let there be no bones made about it – while Skinner mentions the *Liber Spirituum*, precisely the same phase of ritual is concerned in the making of pacts when properly understood. As has been shown elsewhere, pact processes frequently mirror the *Book of Spirits* in all particulars, if indeed the resemblance is not the other way around. The spirit is sworn to various particulars, including to come again when called in future by a simpler formula, an agreement and form which may require some negotiating, though the operator is recommended to have an outline already worked out.

Licensia

As said elsewhere and reiterated by Skinner, the term 'banishing', as opposed to License, is not used traditionally. The License to Depart on the other hand is an essential part of traditional rites; Crowley's preferred form is tolerably similar to that of the *Grimorium Verum*, (as well as containing significant eschatological connotations) but equivalent formulae are frequent in many grimoires.

In the ordinary way, the Magician dismisses the spirit with these words: 'And now I say unto thee, depart in peace unto thine habitations and abodes – and may the blessing of the Highest be upon thee in the name of (here mention the divine name suitable to the operation, or a Name appropriate to redeem that spirit); and let there be peace between thee and me; and be thou very ready to come, whensoever thou art invoked and called; either by a word, or by a will, or by this mighty Conjuration of Magick Art'. ('Magick in Theory and Practice', p. 238, from *Magick: Liber ABA, book four, parts I-IV* by Aleister Crowley, published 1994, Samuel Weiser, Inc.)

Having introduced the 'Classical Frame' I wish now to compare it with another, which it greatly resembles. This in order to show that 'modernism' and 'classicism' are not necessarily airtight compartments, and thus to widen the field of discourse while simultaneously keeping it focused.

Modern Ceremonial Frame: 'best practice'

This is the ritual frame that I employed for a great many years. Some of the externals from previous times may have fallen by the wayside, but I remain familiar with, and respectful of the essentials. While rarely spelt out, and thus liable to lapses, examples of this pattern or frame can often be found wherever Golden Dawn and Crowley's influence is present. This may include modern forms of witchcraft and other occult groups not overtly associated with either. Crowley's *Magick In Theory and Practice* Ch XIII-XVII deals with them in detail. These are its stages:

Banishings

Purifications

Consecrations

Oath & Confession

Invocations

Charge to the Spirit

Closing

Crowley's account of each of these stages is recommended and could be usefully compared with Skinner's. Their essential identity is clear, despite Crowley's tendency to over-allegorise and to assume more clarity in 'modern' thought regarding the process than is perhaps the case. Although the material is less familiar to the 'occult community' than it ought to be, for present purposes I will assume ready access to, or existing familiarity with, this ritual structure. I wish mostly to indicate clearly and simply that it is one, with a few remarks underlining important themes, and leave the practical occultist to absorb and apply it, rather than argue a case which appears self-evident.

The Preparatory Stages of Ritual

BANISHINGS

This involves much more than such rituals as the Lesser Ritual of the Pentagram, or modern in-context equivalents. Indeed, there is no necessity to involve them in consideration of the underlying intent and its role. It is important to acknowledge that while this may be called a 'banishing', its method and, more importantly, its purpose is to invoke protective powers to guard and protect a ritual space or Circle, or indeed the instruments or operator. In context of the pentagram, names of God and angels are invoked, although the format has precedents involving pagan gods associated with the directions. In short, existing ancient and modern analogies abound, and the precise identity of the guardians via sympathetic or hostile theologies is not worthy of overmuch emphasis, structurally speaking.

All this said, the initial banishings of modern ceremonial rituals are not all that is implied. Crowley, rightfully and usefully, places the banishings and purifications in the same chapter. Indeed, his whole discussion of the stages of ritual directly implies that the analysis extends further than Golden Dawn rites and their derivative forms. Rather than simply merging the ideas of 'banishing' and purification, we can perhaps distinguish them by context. Banishing covers various pre-ritual observances, be they the removal of mundane attire before the ritual bath, simply clearing the ritual space prior to use, or the removal of impurities from materials like wax and clay, and many other such examples. Purification meanwhile refers to 'in ritual' formal actions and formulae, such as sprinkling the Circle or a ritual item with lustral water.

A POSTSCRIPT. To consider the banishing rituals of modern ceremonial to have no traditional underpinning, however, would be very rash. The following instructions were included in Reginald Scot's widely consulted compendium, *The Discoverie of Witchcraft*, from 1584.

Of Magical Circles, and the reason of their Institution.

Magitians, and the more learned sort of conjurers, make use of Circles in various manners, and to various intentions. First, when convenience serves not, as to time or place that a real Circle should be delineated, they frame an imaginary Circle, by means of Incantations and Consecrations, without either Knife, Pensil, or Compasses, circumscribing nine foot of ground round about them, which they pretend to sanctifie with words and Ceremonies, spattering their Holy Water all about so far as the said Limit extendeth; and with a form of Consecration following, do alter the property of the ground, that from common (as they say) it becomes sanctifi'd, and made fit for Magicall uses.

How to consecrate an imaginary Circle

Let the Exorcist, being cloathed with a black Garment, reaching to his knee, and under that a white Robe of fine Linnen that falls unto his ankles, fix himself in the midst of that place where he intends to perform his Conjurations: And throwing his old Shooes about ten yards from the place, let him put on his consecrated shooes of russet Leather with a Cross cut un the top of each shooe. Then with his Magical Wand, which must be a new hazel-stick, about two yards of length, he must stretch out his arm to all the four Windes thrice, turning himself round at every Winde, and saying all that while with fervency:

'I who am the servant of the Highest, do by the vertue of his Holy Name Immanuel, sanctifie unto my self the circumference of nine foot round about me, + + +. from the East, Glaurah; from the West, Garron; from the North, Cabon; from the South, Berith; which ground I take for my proper defence from all malignant spirits, that they may have no power over my soul or body, nor come beyond these Limitations, but answer truly being summoned, without daring to transgress their bounds: Worrah. worrah harcot. Gambalon. ✠✠✠.'

Which Ceremonies being perfomed, the place so sanctified is equivalent to any real Circle whatsoever.

Nor is the drawing of symbols in the air during incantations without due precedent in the grimoires. Frequently encountered in this role is the equal-armed cross. Instructions to draw the triangle and – of course – the pentagram in the same way arise on many occasions in the literature. This digression was necessary to demonstrate that uninformed rejection of modern methods on 'traditional grounds' occasionally goes too far, closing doors it were better to have opened.

PURIFICATIONS

Primarily then, this term indicates the 'asperging' with holy water, prepared and employed in a standard, formal manner. This might be in a form from the Catholic Church, or simply following Huson's manual, *Mastering Witchcraft*. Context aside, this is a purging of negative influences, with recognisable ceremonial examples in a variety of sources. Examples, not to simply imitate, but to demonstrate their universality and assist identification, follow.

- À la Huson: 'Water & Earth, where thee art cast, no spell nor adverse purpose last, not in complete accord with me, as my word so mote it be!'
- Thelemic: 'Pure will unassuaged of purpose, delivered from the lust of result, is every way perfect.'
- Modern Ceremonial (from the Chaldean Oracles): 'So therefore first that priest who governeth the works of Fire must sprinkle with the lustral waters of the loud resounding Sea.'
- *Grimorium Verum*: 'Arise, O ye creature of the N to thy baptism of thy pure virtues and service to those operations concerning spirits.'
- Suggested PGM/Oracles cosmology variant: In the Names of Helios and Hecate, I purify this Circle (or Instrument, etc.) by Water.

CONSECRATIONS

A similar format to the previous stage is common and recommended: replacing water with incense, or occasionally anointing oil. The emphasis too is different; it is to sanctify, rather than to cleanse. This is a more active form of protection and empowerment; essentially it is a dedication or making sacred. Again, the same process is also found in minor operations, such as preparation of tools, rather than being restricted to the context of full-scale ritual with conjurations.

- À la Huson: 'Creature of fire this charge I lay, no phantom in thy presence stay. Hear my will addressed to thee; and as my word so mote it be!'
- Thelemic: 'I am uplifted in thine heart; and the kisses of the stars rain hard upon thy body.'
- Modern Ceremonial (from the Chaldean Oracles): 'When after all the phantoms have vanished, thou shalt see that holy and formless fire, that fire which darts and flashes through the

hidden depths of the Universe, hear thou the Voice of Fire.'
- *Grimorium Verum*: 'Angels of God be our help and may our work be accomplished by you. ZALAY, SALMAY, DALMAY, ANGRECTON, LEDRION, AMISOR, EUCHEY, OR. Great Angels: and do thou also, O Adonay, come and give to this a virtue so that this creature [N] may gain a shape, and by this let our work be accomplished. In the name of the Father, and of the Son, and of the Holy Spirit. Amen.'
- Suggested PGM/Oracles cosmology variant: In the Names of Helios and Hecate, I consecrate this Circle (or Instrument, etc.) by Fire.

SUMMARY OF PREPARATORY STAGES

These three stages are the preliminaries of a major rite, when the circle, and all in it, are understood to be concerned. Similar stages may also be found in preliminary works on a smaller scale; for instance, when preparing a particular object or instrument, sometimes in the context of a larger rite, other times outside it. Very similar principles apply, and as preliminary stages, an Opening Ritual may well contain all three as one. This is important to understand as it will facilitate comparison with the older ritual format discussed above.

An excellent example of this 'three in one' preparatory ritual is the 'Opening of the Pyramid' (see *Liber Pyramidos*, Hadean Press, 2010), where all three stages are present in one 'sub-ritual', even though no pentagrams and such are drawn – an important consideration when comparing this structure with older examples.

This, an Opening ritual, involving invocations of protective forces, lustration with specially prepared water and the use of aromatics, precedes the next stage, which involves a very distinct shift of emphasis.

FROM PREPARATION TO DEDICATION

In some examples from the past, this stage is perhaps so much taken as a given it is simply alluded to ('do the usual') or omitted altogether. In others, it has been more clearly identified, but also accumulated elements such as the making of quasi Masonic Grade Signs and the rehearsing of magical names and titles, elements which are obviously peripheral to the main purpose. This purpose is, stating clearly what your intention is in this ritual – hence one of its names, the 'Statement of Intent'. A more traditional sounding name is, 'the Oath', and with it, the Confession.

THE OATH AND CONFESSION

In terms of headings this is the fourth stage of this ritual frame, though in his analysis Crowley calls it the third, presumably due to his connecting banishings and purifications in his analysis, which is legitimate enough. It is more important to note that it is the central stage, a movement onward from the completed preparations and towards the work itself.

The 'Statement of Intent', or more properly the Oath, is a commonplace prayer by comparison, and so it is better to focus here on the Confession as its indispensable corollary.

It is a frequent modern error to omit this stage, or to reduce it to a mere 'statement of intent' without the moral or spiritual implications of either an Oath or a Confession. It is altogether noteworthy that an 'amoral' magician like Crowley makes no such mistake. In the course of his discussion he goes so far as to enjoin prostration, a rare exception to his firm injunctions against even kneeling. It will be seen too, in Crowley's discussion of it, how he anticipates the magician leaping to their feet at the climax of the Confession. This is a clear indication that he has *Pyramidos* very much in mind, which adds to the value of these particular passages for our purposes.

The Confession is and has always been an indispensable aspect of goetic ritual. While certainly present in the grimoire tradition, it far predates any association with the religions 'of the Book'. Without it the magician, or perhaps more clearly, the conjuror, is almost bound to fail or to be deceived. The clearest example of its pagan roots is the role of the 'Negative Confession' in the Egyptian *Book of the Dead*, upon which the form in *Pyramidos* is based. The concept is as at home in Orphic tradition, with their Dionysian subtext – to be precise, the very people Plato indicates in his references to goetia.

INVOCATIONS

This stage is the central one, both in practice and literally, being preceded by three and succeeded by three others. In this the symbolic and the literal are in harmony, appropriately enough. It is a complex phase, and again some credit is due to Aleister Crowley for getting much of it right, in particular his inclusion in the *Goetia*, of the so called Bornless, or more properly Headless Rite, which he significantly and rightly refers to as 'the Preliminary Invocation'. So far as our analysis of ritual mechanics is concerned, objections that it formed no part of the original text, that the ritual was originally an exorcism, and disagreements over the precise identity of the god invoked are of no consequence. What *is* consequential is that it is a preliminary invocation, preceding all others, which invokes a god who can compel any and all other spirits. This is, and always has been, an essential feature of such rituals, a feature few involved in the revival of magic in our times have acknowledged. The other matters above listed are details, interesting enough in other contexts, but this context exceeds them in significance.

In short, the Invocations should begin with the invoking of such an intermediary. In the context of goetic ritual this usually means a power of the East under various names, exceeding all the others in authority. Their authority may derive from a still loftier part of the hierarchy, but the central fact remains. In the *Grimorium Verum* – unlike other grimoires in a less complete or more garbled state – this entity, and more importantly their role, is clearly identified. Moreover, in the ritual as given, his invocation is preceded by a ritual offering of Mace, a fiery and mercurial fume, appropriate not simply to him, but identifiable as of the same nature as many gods with this role, in many cultures over many thousands of years (Agni, Girru, Hermes, etc.).

After this invocation, others follow, usually more specific to the precise entity. For example, in *Verum* again, invocations of the appropriate Chief and then the appropriate deputy of that Chief follow, preceding the conjuration of the particular spirit or spirits required. This 'Chain of Command' process is to be contrasted with the 'thwarting angel' approach, which has traditional precedents is only one form, rather than a universal one. For some reason Skinner details this ahead of an analysis of the ritual stages, whereas discussions of this kind really belong to the Invocations specifically. Unlike the role of the Intermediary, thwarting angels (for example, those of the *Shemhamphorash*) are not a master key to all rituals. They are a variant aspect of an adaptation of the process to a monotheistic and dualistic approach.

The subject of intermediaries is examined in some detail in my *Testament of Cyprian the Mage*. Such a role is not restricted to either pagan gods or to demonic princes; there are particular 'angelic' intermediaries also. This reflects the mythological analogues of ritual processes, since there is more than one 'type' who can fulfil this role, the 'Angelic Viceregent' being one. Thus, in various rites of the past and present, a major Archangel, frequently Michael, operates in precisely this role.

A further note on invocations worth adding in conclusion is that many stages of ritual – other than the invocations themselves – **may** include an invocation. In modern magic, for example, banishing rituals also include brief invocations of the angels. So too purifications and consecrations may include brief invocations of a suitable god or angel. Just as an important form of the more extended invocation incudes building up an image of a god by rehearsing their attributes, so can the briefer form. So, for instance, in *Pyramidos*, prior to the magician purifying and anointing themselves, Tahuti is invoked thus:

O thou the apex of the plane
With Ibis head and Phoenix wand,
And wings of Night, whose serpents strain
Their bodies bounding the beyond
Thou in the Light and in the Night
Art One above their moving might

This swiftly builds a mental image of the Ibis-headed god, winged and embraced by two serpents (resembling the caduceus), as well as affirming his role and place in the frame of the ritual itself (top point of the triangular floor plan, unifier of the twin forces invoked, etc.).

We also find brief invocations employed in the act of consecrating talismans (see remarks on the Charge to the Spirit), as for example in the grimoire appearing earlier in this work.

THE CHARGE TO THE SPIRIT

Careful readers will note that in the ritual shorthand given earlier, the same symbol used for the Oath is also used to denote the Charge to the Spirit. Crowley's relevant chapters detail this equivalence, and this explains to a degree why the literal meaning of 'conjure' is 'to swear together'. Naturally enough the 'statement of intent' refers to the magician's desires, and in the Charge to the Spirit these requirements are repeated. Above and beyond this, the magician and the spirit recognise the same sources of authority. Thus, the names of power employed by the magician are as significant to the spirit as the operator, and at appropriate points in the rite both parties swear by them either implicitly or explicitly.

One of Crowley's significant insights into the process outlined here is that another form of the Charge to the Spirit is the Talisman. This clarifies the close relationship talismanic magic has with the ritual processes of conjuration; they are two forms of magic which are very frequently encountered alongside – with interchangeable parts – in various grimoires. That the underlying conception is the same, and the ritual processes essentially similar (give or take an Order of Magnitude), is not difficult to see. One subtle implication of this is that a great deal may be learned, relatively safely, regarding conjuration by experimenting extensively with its structural principles first in works of talismanic magic. With experience, the same principles may readily be applied to working with spirits in spell work in general, particularly as the most effective spells require a material form, readily comparable with talismans.

CLOSING

As said previously under the *Licensia* section of Frame 1, actual banishing rituals are not required for the same phase to be implied. The License to Depart however is an essential part of formal ritual procedure. The Closing by *Pyramidos* however gives a more elaborate procedure, which may be concluded with the License to Depart or possibly preceded by them depending on the nature of the spirits involved. This resembles the Opening in most respects, which as discussed already is equivalent to the *Consecratio Dei*. It can be readily assumed from this that this closing process is certainly thorough.

There is one principle difference from both the *Pyramidos* Opening and the 'Ruddian' frame. This is the presence within it of a Eucharistic ritual, specifically a 'Mass of the Four Elements'. While introduced seemingly via Golden Dawn principles, though an older source is possible, this is well worth retaining for a variety of reasons.

Firstly, retaining and developing the priestly capacity of the magician required or 'given' in grimoire and pre-Christian era rites, whether fashionable or not, is a strategic necessity.

Secondly, and following from the first, the principles of 'Restitutionism', or more simply 'elevating the spirits' – those who are invited to participate in the closing, when the License is given afterward – have a share in the elements of the Mass.

Thirdly, simple practicality is served, as for instance when a stone or other item is required for a rite or spell, over which a Mass or indeed series of Masses has been said.

Frames compared

The major job of comparison between the 'Ruddian' and the 'Crowleyan' stages has been attended to in the process of delineating them. Application requires a little more attention. The shorthand form of the outline (pentagram, triangles, square, etc.) was useful to me many years back when working with both modern and traditional rituals. After writing the symbols in a column, I could then sketch out a ritual, or indeed examine an existing one. Ritual components, as for example a purification ritual, could be slotted together, missing components identified and replaced, and so on. While at one time I generally did use banishing rituals, the other components were more often taken from older sources, including the grimoires, the Leyden Papyrus and so forth. In short, I was assuming, as Skinner does of a slightly different form, that this outline was a useful standard and effective tool. I did not suppose it to be spectacularly ancient – after all, I had found it in Crowley who presumably got it from the Golden Dawn or related source. I simply found it an incredibly useful approach to ritual composition, reconstruction, and analysis.

Now, it is a fact that Crowley was familiar with some of Rudd's materials; for example, they are the source of the geomantic correspondences to the Enochian alphabet that occur in his *Vision and the Voice*. Nor need this surprise us: Frederick Hockley, a 'predecessor' of the Golden Dawn respected by Wynn Westcott and others, was instrumental in maintaining the literary tradition of the grimoires, including texts attributed to Rudd. Rudd-derived materials influenced Golden Dawn Enochiania, in and out of the core texts of that society. In short, it is very possible and even likely that Crowley's ritual structure in *Magick in Theory and Practice* derives, directly, or indirectly, from the same text Skinner examines and approves. The purported distance between modern and traditional magic is considerably reduced when this is considered. There remains the possibility that Rudd himself is a literary invention of one Peter Smart, or a composite wish fulfilment figure involving more than one bearer of the Rudd name. This leaves delightfully open the whole question of whether proven traditional authenticity really matters as much as efficacy.

Appendix II: Matters Sacerdotal or Lineage, Accidental and Deliberate

While my feelings and thoughts regarding it are clear enough, this is perhaps the most difficult section of this book to write. It is also the most likely to be misunderstood in various ways. Yet the matter cannot be avoided, although perhaps it may be simplified somewhat, and abstruse aspects rendered less opaque. Difficult though the topic may be, the best recourse is to bite the bullet and begin.

The religion of the grimoires

There is no doubting that the grimoires as we receive them are Christian, even though heterodox elements abound. Similarly, at least a proportion of those writing and using them were not merely Christians but clerics. This should not greatly surprise us; the term 'ritual specialists' has been applied to pagan and other magicians of earlier times – such expertise is more native to a priest whatever their religion.

In the period of the grimoires this expertise, quite naturally, was often associated with Catholic clerics, although the subsequent successful adaptations of the methodology by Reformation intellectuals should not be understated (see *An Excellent Book* in the bibliography). One might compare the major role that Catholic iconography and liturgy has played in New World traditions, while similarly recognising that the Christian element in Hoodoo, for example, though possessing African roots is primarily Protestant. Nor should we overlook the Orthodox and even Pagan currents at work in the Byzantine grimoires, nor the Arab Hermeticism of the *Picatrix*. Nevertheless, in the folk traditions of Europe, as well as the more literary magic of the grimoires, a very major proportion of the structure and inspiration, the iconography and the forms of words, are Catholic, heterodox and subject to persecution though it was. So too, as indicated, the traditions of the African diaspora in the New World involve the same admixture. In short, whatever its primal roots, for upwards of two thousand years magic has drawn upon Christianity to provide coherence and 'frames'. Such coherence and facility are not readily retained in an eclectic mish-mash, such as we see in all too many modern occult works.

From Protestant to Pagan

In the current time there are various issues in the occult mass mind which primers, and indeed most other works, have yet to address. While I do not feel like the most suitable person to address them, there is something to be said for at least acknowledging one or two – just raising the subject, as it were.

For example, there is the fact that the 'occult revivals' of 1875 and 1975 took place within a largely Protestant/post-Protestant and Anglophone culture. Key players may have answered to no such description (one thinks of Gurdjeff and Blavatsky); predecessor revivals in – say – Catholic France certainly deserve renewed historical consideration. However, the major demographic, and the culture most influenced, certainly matches the description. Consciously or otherwise Anglophone (Post) Protestant culture has influenced our collective thinking, and either helped or hindered any emergent esoteric worldview.

Also, the early magical revival – as distinct from the more Orientalist Theosophical movement – was if not nominally Christian, at least Rosicrucian (which, opinions to the contrary notwithstanding, was in inception also a Protestant movement). However, this late 19th century strand was not to dominate modern magic alone. The later phase of the revival saw neo-paganism eclipse neo-masonic frames and narratives. Friends recently spoke of neopaganism as currently the dominant 'syncretising' force at work in modern occulture, an observation not far from the truth. Thus it is that I speak of a particular mindset or collective within modern occultism as going from Protestant to Pagan, with all the attendant limitations and cultural blind-spots that brings with it.

Simply to recognise this in a retrospective historical fashion may be semi-useful, but without doing more, it remains problematic. So, a forward-looking modern primer may legitimately raise the subject and propose tactics and strategies suited to this situation in order to facilitate further progress, insight and positive outcomes from it – tactics and strategies framed on magical principles, rather than in accord with theological or political fashions.

Introducing Jack

In previous phases of modern Anglophone occultism, to have openly admitted that your first major intimation of magic, in the here and now, was through contact with an ancestor during illness, would have had varied receptions. Suspicions of overt spiritualist tendencies would render various magical factions uneasy, from the Golden Dawn founders to an early Chaos Magician (mentioning no names). Attitudes towards so-called 'primitive beliefs' would once have placed such anecdotes beyond the pale. Today of course, some might still suspect mental illness, or attribute physiological causes in a mechanistic fashion. Nevertheless, this was the case with your current author.

To be specific, I was in intensive care as a child, and being kept under observation, when a grandfather who had died before I was born made himself known. A few recollected details he revealed about himself – or that I somehow absorbed through the contact – have been substantiated, and other interesting facts have come to light. I mention this in advance of relevant details because the connection with our current theme did not emerge at once, and other things require discussion. My major impression initially was simply that I was not going to die, and that there was a continuity between him and me that was somehow significant to the life I had yet to lead. I also, somehow, knew he was a member of a druidic Order – whose current form is of no interest to me – and other affiliations duly came to light, some of more interest than others, as shall be seen.

Ritual Specialists

The involvement of priests in the composing and performance of the grimoires has been mentioned. That it is not an all-encompassing involvement to the exclusion of other possibilities is worth keeping in mind, but nonetheless, the matter has ramifications. The Christianity of the genre, heterodox or no, is also a given. This does not mean that analogies with other traditions, where myth and ritual mechanics overlap, even coincide, are nonapplicable – quite the contrary. The *theology* of the grimoires, again, heterodox or no, can thus be understood as a *technology*. While understanding it this way may not come naturally to moderns, it appears to have been perfectly straightforward to the grimoirists. The cleric, as expert technician, was thus endowed with special abilities. To be brief rather than comprehensive, these include the ability to perform, to compose and to adapt or rebuild rituals on magical lines. In Catholic tradition and others, though less so in the Orthodox communions, this has various very deep implications. Culturally speaking, clerics are closely related to historical magical practice and indeed to other things, esoteric and otherwise. Nor has the coherent currency and applicability of the ideas concerned here diminished in our time.

Some of my readers will be more familiar with aspects of this topic than others, and some ramifications to follow are likewise patchily distributed. Nor do I particularly favour some of the baggage involved. There is too a potential for abuse and misuse of these ideas, for vain observance, for clubbish-ness. However, tactics and strategies framed on magical principles and appropriate to emerging contexts is what I set out to deliver, and that danger is simply par for the course. Approval or disapproval on non-magical grounds does not impact effectiveness and authenticity in magical terms. Magicians bend the rules, which is considerably more effective when you know them. One might as well criticise a sailor for working at sea as protest this from a magician.

To continue with a more familiar illustration of the principle I am skirting around, to induce understanding rather than lay out a recipe, it is a commonplace motif that the Black Mass, legendary or historical, can 'only' be performed by an unfrocked priest. In practice a willing priest appears to have been an acceptable substitute. In fact, however, the two kinds of priest are magically equivalent, particularly in terms of the given theological understanding.

Episcopi vagantes

A similar understanding pertains precisely in the case of an *episcopus vagans* (singular form, a Latin term, pejorative but useful) which in simple terms denotes a wandering, or stray, bishop.

In traditional usage these are primarily persons consecrated as Christian bishops, particularly in a 'clandestine or irregular way', while outside the structures and canon law of an established church. Also, they are those whose consecration was regular but who were later excommunicated and are not in communion with a recognised diocese; the analogy with the 'Black Mass priest' is here extremely close. They have the consecration; it remains effective despite their having 'wandered'.

In more extended use, the same term has come to represent 'independent' bishops who often 'collect' various lines of transmitted Apostolic Succession. These may extend consecration to others for various motives, financial perhaps, but idealistic and gratis services are not unknown. Although not universal, there is considerable involvement of such ecclesiastics in recent and not so recent occultism, on most continents. The spectrum of 'chivalric orders', quixotic pageantry, and serious occult interests gives the matter a chequered reputation. Again, with magic, such ambivalence is a quality that comes naturally, and serves its purpose better than the cut and dried.

Dragging this into context, in the grimoire period wandering clerics of lesser rank (*clerici vagantes*) would certainly overlap with the 'clerical underground' concerned with the grimoires; literal itineracy as well as figurative might frequently be understood. Apparently, the term for those who recognise no authority, even an antipope or schismatic bishop for example, is *acephali*, a word not without other occult resonance, pleasingly enough. As with the wandering bishops, obviously modern analogues of the *clerici vagantes* are very much extant today, in and out of certain magical orders. My interest has always been framed in terms of utter independence from, rather than close association with, a Masonic structure, and any such connection has no bearing on my raising the matter now.

To conclude, in the Christian West it has been taught, or at very least believed with some justification for centuries, that regardless of the status of either party, any bishop can consecrate any baptised man as a bishop, and that only the minimum requirements need be observed to ensure the sacramental validity of the ceremony. This regardless of whether the consecration respects Church law in certain respects, or whether the participants are in legitimate communion or are schismatic, or outright heretics and magicians.

Like this or loathe this, it certainly has claim to traditional authenticity, is in context with grimoire thinking, and has relevant tactical and strategic implications.

A Digression

At one time I was involved with a highly active magical group, something I had avoided for some years prior, but an exception was justified, suffice it to say. In due course, I came to have some responsibilities within and for it. Despite some laudable detachment from such things by this group, external occult politics eventually intruded. Originally a localised group, which expanded to two centres in the UK, international contacts were also made and a 'sister group' relationship formed with an established independent US sodality. Another, larger, US body became established in the UK a little after this and relations were, occasionally, if unnecessarily, strained for a while, although we shared common interests and individual members of both got along.

In the same time period, the matter of 'Wandering Bishops' became quite topical, even controversial. While not being remotely impressed by Western 'lineages', there were other aspects that carried greater interest. Group forms in modern Western magic had been problematic for some time, with Orders especially. An ecclesiastical model, so to speak, with adherents or sympathisers as congregation, and active or dedicated 'clergy' working sometimes with, sometimes without them, seemed like an alternative with some potential. The matter was not a major concern for me otherwise, but people in the community were talking about it and those were my thoughts.

So, as said, there were some strained relations, and insinuations of non- authenticity or worse by factions in the larger group towards the smaller. All very tiresome, but not a great impediment as such. A publication from that group arrived in the mail in which the ecclesiastical side of things was current, and the chief set forth his personal 'Gnostic' lineage as a matter of some importance at the time. And there, in the midst of the listed so-and-soes ordaining other so-and-soes prior to him, was the name of our sister order's then leader. Almost needless to say, we spoke of this; my vague interest in ecclesiastical lineages quickened somewhat, and my ordination followed, with subsequent additions. My main motives were from responsibility – duty of care – so there was no frivolity concerned.

The initial devious move out of the way, the magical potential of ordination, a priesthood, or even a Church, overcame my remaining resistance quite quickly, if not my distaste for charters and such as measures of authenticity. Or, to put it another way, the ordination 'took' and I began a new if covert life as a bishop who could do bishop things. The transmission of a current so to speak, with various provisions for activation and even reanimation by magical means, by 'ecclesiastic magic', became coherent, doable, and of obvious interest.

Ancestors Resumed

To return to my first ancestral contact and all it entailed, you will recall I mentioned him having a few other affiliations. Among these was the Order of Oddfellows, which has gone through a few transformations from its beginnings, if one had the interest to follow them up. That is not where I'm going at all; Rosicrucian and other Masonic and quasi-masonic certificates unearthed in attics of departed relatives are still reasonably commonplace. No, the most interesting and central affiliation was a 'Church'; a religious movement or group might be a better term.

It was this affiliation most of all which shaped his values and actions, as they had my great-grandfather's too, along with their families and others around them. His influence shaped my father's life, values, and actions too, even though he 'lapsed' from religious attendance in the increasingly secular 1960s. This group – in which both grandfather and great-grandfather were lay preachers – had a name. I use the past tense because that name has changed in a somewhat significant way since, but first some more details.

This movement was founded by James Banyard, in Rochford, Essex, in the year 1838. Banyard was not a theology graduate, but a farm worker's son and a shoemaker. More than this, he was a poacher, possible smuggler, and general troublemaker who frequented disreputable pubs, and jeered at religion openly. Physically unattractive he was nevertheless charismatic and popular, adept in conjuring tricks, mimicry and rhyming. He was also a composer of acapella comedy songs known as 'glees', which one imagines were sung at the same public houses. Habitual drunkenness and time in prison incited his wife, Susan Garnish, to insist he reform; she packed him off to a Wesleyan Church, which proved to be a pivotal and lifechanging event. He duly reformed, and in time became a Wesleyan preacher until in 1837; after some differences which are obscure, he and a partner founded their own church in an old workhouse building called The Barracks. They subsequently moved, establishing their Church in his own cottage in Workhouse Lane.

The name they took for the Church was the Peculiar People – the continuity with Oddfellows does not escape me. They were also referred to as Peculiars or Banyardites. The origins of this name are to be found in both Testaments of the Bible:

Deuteronomy 14:2: For thou art an holy people unto the Lord thy God, and the Lord hath chosen thee to be a peculiar people unto himself, above all the nations that are upon the earth.

1 Peter 2:9 But ye are a chosen generation, a royal
priesthood, an holy nation, a peculiar people; that ye
should shew forth the praises of him who hath called you
out of darkness into his marvellous light.

In the language of the KJV, *peculiar* obviously means special,
not least in this context. The movement, indeed much of Essex, was
staunchly nonconformist, the area being a stronghold of Puritanism
since the reign of Elizabeth I. They were often conscientious
objectors, and also practiced divine healing, which is unusual in
non-Pentecostal Protestantism. This first came about spontaneously,
when William Perry was brought to the barracks weak with
consumption. Perry, praying, had heard a voice reciting a biblical
prayer (James 5: 14-15) and believed the preacher – Banyard –
could act as an instrument of the Lord and heal. Banyard was
initially reluctant, but eventually they knelt together and prayed.
Perry walked twelve miles that same day. Other healings followed,
and the Church grew phenomenally. Banyard was a charismatic
preacher with a thunderous voice, and his unaccompanied singing
of hymns lively.

Sadly, their healing practices, and attendant beliefs, led to
controversy internal and external when children were refused
medicine in consequence of doctrinal rejection of doctors. The
responsibility of parents to provide their children with medical care
came into law through trials in this period. This was an extreme, even
fatal position which Banyard did not support, and he was unbishoped
in the Church he founded because of his position. The movement
was divided over this, with first the extreme 'Old Peculiars', and in
time the more reasonable 'New Peculiar' position prevailing. While
reduced in influence in his own Church, supported by a minority
in the one building he owned, the fact remains nevertheless that
Banyard himself and the early 'Banyardites' did have considerable
success with their healing of adults, which accounted for their early

growth. It was this that had led to the establishment of a formal Constitution and a hierarchy of bishops, elders and 'saints', to cope with their rapid expansion into Kent and East London.

While biblical literalism remained and still does, by the 1950s the divine healing aspect of the movement was receding, although in earlier times it had instead developed from original biblical prayer alone to laying on of hands and other methods. With these modern changes, the movement in which my ancestors partook, two generations of lay preachers and my father included, changed its name – by Deed Poll – to the 'less conspicuous' Union of Evangelical Churches. To be absolutely precise, on the 27th of April 1956, the day upon which I was born, the Peculiar People ceased to be – as such – and your author came into being.

My grandfather, who I never knew in life, was undoubtedly a good man, and his values and actions reflected his Methodist convictions. The Peculiars were credited with helping bring order to Daw's Heath, an area once described as a 'hotbed of lawlessness', which has an active UEC Church to this day. Jack – my grandfather – actively helped encourage young men in the toughest parts of East London to abandon crime and drink and to become musicians, thereby lifting themselves out of the gutter. All his sons too were gifted musicians, and music played an enormous part in their lives.

Personal responsibility was a strong part of the message, which passed through generations of my family on both sides. Methodism indeed – in rural Essex and elsewhere – was 'small c' conservative, but often socially progressive or benign; I have mentioned active conscientious objection, and Wesley himself had visited America and passionately opposed slavery. Wesleyanism in general was a movement of working people and a powerful force for good in some respects, though it is fading from the British, perhaps the world scene nowadays. This is a change for the worse in some ways, even though the earlier unreformed, roistering Banyard and I may have had more in common.

In short, I have no time for the fuss regarding initiations, lineages, charters and associated issues in modern Anglophone occultism, preferring instead the spirit to the dead letter and improved knowledge of our traditions rather than static dogmatism. Circumstances nevertheless made of me an effectively ordained if heterodox bishop, while I inherited ancestral Peculiarity, so to speak, from birth. Should these 'Christian' things be required in a conjuror and modern grimoire liturgist, then I am not without them. If they are not, then my work suffices, as I prefer. Who can determine for certain either way?

BIBLIOGRAPHY AND FURTHER READING

RELATED GRIMOIRES

Agrippa, Cornelius (attrib), *The Fourth Book of Occult Philosophy*
Albertus Magnus (attrib), *Le Petit Albert*, various editions
Albertus Magnus (attrib), *Le Grand Albert*, various editions
Albertus Magnus (attrib), *The Book of the Secrets of Albertus Magnus*, various editions
Betz, Hans Dieter (Editor), *The Greek Magical Papyri in Translation* (University of Chicago Press, 1986, 1992)
Driscoll, D.J., *The Sworn Book of Honourius the Magician* (Heptangle Books, 1977)
Malchus, Marius, *The Secret Grimoire of Turiel* (Aquarian Press, 1960, 1971)
Peterson, Joseph, *The Clavis or Key to the Magic of Solomon* (Ibis, 2009)
Peterson, Joseph, *Arbatel – Concerning the Magic of the Ancients* (2009)

RITUAL STRUCTURE

Crowley, Aleister, *Magick in Theory and Practice* (aka *Magick* or *Liber ABA* part III)
Skinner, Stephen and Rankine, David, Eds. *The Goetia of Doctor Rudd* (Golden Hoard Press, 2010)

MATTERS SACERDOTAL

Legard, P. and Cummins, A., *An Excellent Booke of the Arte of Magicke* (Scarlet Imprint. 2020)

FURTHER READING

Betz, Hans Dieter, 'Fragments from a Catabasis Ritual in a Greek Magical Papyrus', *History of Religions*, 19.4 (May 1980) 287-295

Griffiths, F.L. and Thompson, H., Eds., *The Leyden Papyrus* (Dover Publications, 1974)

Huson, Paul, *Mastering Witchcraft* (G.P. Putnams, 1970)

Peterson., Joseph, Twilit Grotto: CD with Search Engine, and online archive: http://www.esotericarchives.com

Stratton-Kent, Jake, *The True Grimoire* (Scarlet Imprint, 2009)

Stratton-Kent, Jake, *Geosophia – The Argo of Magic* (Scarlet Imprint, 2010)

Stratton-Kent, Jake, *The Testament of Cyprian the Mage* (Scarlet Imprint, 2014)

Stratton-Kent, Jake, *Pandemonium: A Discordant Concordance of Diverse Spirit Catalogues* (Hadean Press, 2016)

INDEX